D0436862

Also by Marcella Hazan

The Classic Italian Cook Book
More Classic Italian Cooking
Marcella's Italian Kitchen
Essentials of Classic Italian Cooking
Marcella Cucina
Marcella Says . . .
Amarcord: Marcella Remembers

INGREDIENTI

*Marcella's Guide
to the Market*

MARCELLA HAZAN

and

VICTOR HAZAN

Illustrated by
Karin Kretschmann Lubart

SCRIBNER

New York   London   Toronto   Sydney   New Delhi

SCRIBNER
An Imprint of Simon & Schuster, Inc.
1230 Avenue of the Americas
New York, NY 10020

First Scribner hardcover edition July 2016

SCRIBNER and design are registered trademarks of The Gale Group, Inc.,
used under license by Simon & Schuster, Inc., the publisher of this work.

For information about special discounts for bulk purchases,
please contact Simon & Schuster Special Sales at 1-866-506-1949
or business@simonandschuster.com.

The Simon & Schuster Speakers Bureau can bring authors to your live event.
For more information or to book an event, contact the Simon & Schuster Speakers
Bureau at 1-866-248-3049 or visit our website at www.simonspeakers.com.

Interior design by Erich Hobbing

Manufactured in the United States of America

1   3   5   7   9   10   8   6   4   2

Library of Congress Cataloging-in-Publication Data is available.

ISBN 978-1-4516-2736-7
ISBN 978-1-4516-2737-4 (ebook)

In the mornings of the last two years of her life, after taking one more sip from the very large cup that I had filled for her with espresso, Marcella went to her desk where she let her thoughts loose in the food markets she had known, bringing them again to the products on which her gaze had stopped, products which, in her kitchen, she could transform into dishes of haunting deliciousness and stunning simplicity. She set her thoughts down in a tight, round, feminine hand, filling the pages of lined notebooks. She wrote in Italian, rarely stopping to revise, moving quickly to the end of a line, as though to stay ahead of time's encroaching passage.

I translated and organized those pages. As the only member of this partnership left standing, I shall exercise my right to pen a dedication. This guide is the testament of a woman who based her cooking life on the truth of every dish she cooked and taught, the vigorous truth of clear, uncluttered taste, taste that arises neither from obeisance to dogma, nor from a craving for attention, but evolves inspired by, and respectful of, the ingredients that nourish it. To that woman I dedicate this work.

To Marcella.

CONTENTS

THE ESSENTIAL PANTRY

SALUMI

WHAT AM I DOING HERE?

Victor Hazan

For sixty years of an inseparable relationship, Marcella had a partner. A sometimes, but not always, silent partner, a partner standing by in her kitchen, a partner for her daily explorations of the food market, a partner in the conversations about cooking that were an indivisible part of dining at home and out, a partner to give her Italian prose English expression. I was, and continue to be, that partner.

Marcella's passion was teaching. She had studied to become a teacher, and in her youth she taught mathematics and the biological sciences. Marriage revealed her genius for cooking and, in the latter half of a long life, cooking is what she taught. She wrote this book knowing it would be her final opportunity to guide other cooks toward the most desirable choice of ingredients, to share with them her knowledge, her methods, and her thoughts in producing what she viewed as one of the richest sources of contentment: good home cooking.

Anyone who has cooked with Marcella will recall her saying: "Don't think so much about what else you can put into a recipe. What you keep out is just as important as what you put in." There are dishes, of course, that benefit from a copious variety of ingredients. The minestrone that Marcella used to make for us could contain a dozen vegetables or more. She packed her books, however, with recipes listing no more than five ingredients, often even fewer. Her famous tomato sauce that traveled the world has only three. In recent years, simple cooking has become a frequently cited ideal. Cooks and food writers often talk about it. Marcella practiced it. She was a tireless defender of the respect that was owed ingredients. "If you have something fresh and wonderful cooking in the pan, don't crowd it with herbs and spices and other odd companions; give it room. Let it speak out."

Marcella wrote in Italian, fast, without hesitation, leaving no space between lines, filling several legal-size notebooks with her manuscript. She concentrated on such ingredients as you can buy without assistance, on produce, on pantry items, on salumi. Excluded therefore are seafood and meat, for whose purchase you depend on the cooperation of a reliable fishmonger or butcher. The ingredients that she describes are those that you'd be likely to find in our kitchen. They are associated with Italian cooking because that is what Marcella did, but they are common in everyday cooking for many cuisines.

She loved this project and dedicated to it the customary passion with which she worked. It took me a long while to fortify myself, to open her notebooks, to read that familiar hand. This became the last tribute I could offer, to give her book its English-speaking voice. I have worked alone in the kitchen where Marcella reigned, and I have been testing recipes with many of the ingredients she discusses here. It is remarkable how well her simple approach works. Every day of our life that Marcella and I ate at home—and that accounted for most of our days—Marcella cooked a fresh, satisfying meal. With the insight into ingredients that she provides here, good cooks should be capable of using her as their model, to invest the taste of their own cooking with the clarity that is Marcella's.

INGREDIENTI

HOW I FELL IN LOVE
WITH INGREDIENTS

Marcella Hazan

A few months after Victor and I were married, we moved from my hometown of Cesenatico, in Emilia-Romagna, to New York. My husband began to work in his family's business in the city; I stayed at home and began to cook. I had trained for a teaching career in science. Cooking was something I was doing for the first time. I was doing it in a place far from my own family and friends, stumbling over a language I had never before spoken, shopping in markets whose products were baffling to me.

I had an Italian cookbook, and a few recipes that my mother had sketched out for me. They did not, however, open the door to where I needed to go. It wasn't to cooking methods that I directed most of my thoughts in the kitchen. Common sense and a few trials quickly made those clear to me. The ultimate object of my attention wasn't the pot on the stove as much as the food at the table. What interested me was taste. I searched my memory for the flavors, textures, and scents of the food I had grown up with in Italy. Once I could bring the taste of a dish into focus, I was able to choose the ingredients that were most congenial to that taste. Or, vice versa, if I found myself drawn to an ingredient that I found in the market, I let it suggest the dish I could make with it.

Cooking had quickly developed into an important part of my husband's life and mine, and my relationship with ingredients became a close one. I thought about them, even when I wasn't shopping for them. I thought about their fragrance, their color, their texture, their flavor. In the market, I loved to pick them up, which I would not have been permitted to do at any produce stall in Italy, inspect them, test their firmness, admire their freshness, smell them.

There have been no more satisfying times in my life than those that I have spent in a food market, wherever in the world I have been. The colors, shapes, and fragrances that drew me to the stalls aroused thoughts upon thoughts of the pleasures I might bring out of my kitchen. In my mind, I have conceived more dishes in an hour or two in the market than I could ever have produced in any one mealtime at home.

Looking for ingredients should be more deliberate than dropping them into your basket and checking them off a shopping list. Think of this book as a collection of portraits. Each wants to be a description of character. Become familiar with them, establish a connection, and allow them to guide you to making food that you enjoy and will be pleased to share.

PRODUCE

Gli Ortaggi

Baby, spiny, and globe artichokes

ARTICHOKES

I Carciofi

I have never boiled an artichoke. There are cooks, I understand, who have never made artichokes any other way. What a pity. Artichokes possess more fascinating ways to please than almost any other vegetable. Just on their own, they can be sautéed, braised, fried, or grilled; they can be delicious sliced very thin and eaten raw with lemon juice and olive oil. They can be used in a risotto, a frittata, a soup, terrific lasagna, a rustic torta, a gratin, a stew. Cooking them is not at all complicated. Prepping them, however, is indisputably an exercise in patience, particularly so with the small ones.

There are two basic varieties of artichokes grown for the American market. One of these, the globe, is round in shape as its name suggests. The leaves, which have a small indentation at their tip, curl tightly inward. They are almost always available, but their ideal season is from very late winter to early summer. The globe resembles the Italian artichoke known as *mammola* in Rome, where it is often served *alla giudia*, flattened and fried to a crisp, its leaves curling in imitation of a chrysanthemum.

The other variety is smaller than the globe. Its leaves, which are often purplish, lean slightly outward with a thorn at their tip. Their flavor is more intensely artichokey than that of the mild-mannered globe.

Small artichokes, whose growers describe them as babies, have made a welcome entry into the market. They come from the same plant as the larger ones, but they are clipped from a lower section. They don't have a fuzzy choke at their heart, and they have a fine taste, but they require at least as much patience to prep thoroughly as the larger ones.

When you are about to buy artichokes, look them over carefully to be sure that they are fresh and worth the effort you'll be putting into preparing them. Bend back a leaf, which should snap, not fold over limply. Check the bottom end of the stem where it has been cut. It should still be green and possibly dewy, at least in part. If it is dark or even black and lifeless, it was cut from the plant too long ago. Keep fresh artichokes for up to a week in the refrigerator, stowed in a large open plastic bag. Baby artichokes are usually sold in a plastic box in which you can refrigerate them for about a week.

When you are ready to prep them, set the following equipment out on your counter: a half lemon, a bowl of water into which you've squeezed the other half of the lemon, a sharp chef's knife, a paring knife or grapefruit spoon, a vegetable peeler with a swiveling blade (sometimes called a Y peeler), and a large empty bowl or a trash can for the discards.

Begin by holding the artichoke bulb by its base. Press the thumb of one hand against the base of a leaf; with the other hand grasp the tip of the leaf and pull it sharply back against the thumb of the first hand, snapping off the leaf just above its paler base—do not remove the base because it's a desirable part of the artichoke; go around the bulb snapping away leaf by leaf until you have exposed a pale-colored central cone dark only at its tip; using the chef's knife, cut off the top of the cone leaving just its pale base; with the half lemon rub the cut edges of the artichoke to keep them from getting dark.

You are now able to look into the artichoke's center, where there is a ring of soft, tiny leaves with prickly tips that curve inward. Use the tip of the paring knife or the grapefruit spoon to scrape them away along with the fuzzy choke beneath them. Do not carve away any part of the artichoke's tender and delicious bottom. Take a last look at the outside of the bulb, where you see the stumps of the leaves you snapped away. If you spot any remaining dark green part, pare it away now.

If you are making artichokes Roman style, in which the full stem remains attached to the bulb, leave the stem on. For other preparations, detach it, but do not discard it, because it is very good to eat. Cut off a quarter-inch disk from the stem's bottom. A dark green layer sheathes the stem's pale core. The core is tender and delectable, but the outer dark green layer is tough and stringy and must be stripped completely away with the paring knife or vegetable peeler. Drop the trimmed bulb and stem in the bowl of lemony water, and continue until you have prepped all your artichokes. Keep large trimmed artichokes in the water up to a few hours before you cook them. If you are working with baby artichokes, you can keep them for at least a week in the refrigerator. Pack them as close as possible in a glass jar with half a squeezed lemon, and fill the jar to overflowing with lemony water. Screw the cap on tightly.

Victor's note: In the last week of her life, Marcella prepped an entire box of baby artichokes. They are in the refrigerator in a glass jar where they are to remain.

ARUGULA

La Rucola

Find a forager and ask for wild arugula. It brings a salad to life. It will bring your palate to life. Foraged arugula was the only kind one used to buy in Italian markets. Black-robed old women with aprons tied at their waists used to hunt for it in the country alongside irrigation ditches where it often grew. They cupped their aprons and, when they bulged with arugula and possibly some *radicchietto*, they would head home, empty the aprons, and if they had a strong back, head to the ditches for more. When they had had enough, they would sell what they had collected at the market stall that handled greens.

You would need only a few leaves of nutty and explicitly peppery wild arugula to accent a large salad. If you don't have a forager connection, the arugula that you'll be bringing back from the farmers' market or the store is a cultivated green that comes in two forms, either large or small. They are both mild in taste, but the smaller is prettier. The larger leaves have tough stems, which must be cut off.

Wash arugula in a large basin of cold water. Scoop up the leaves, pour the water out, refill the basin, then put the arugula back in. Repeat the procedure until you see no more dirt settling to the bottom of the basin. Retrieve the arugula leaves, and if you are using them shortly in a salad, spin them dry in a salad spinner. If you are going to use them at another time, place them on a layer of paper towels and spread another layer of paper towels on top. Press firmly, but gently, to absorb as much moisture as possible. Wrap the arugula in a fresh sheet of paper towels, place it in a large resealable plastic bag, close the bag, and store it in the vegetable drawer of the refrigerator. In a really cold refrigerator it will keep in good condition for as long as ten days.

Arugula

ASPARAGUS

Gli Asparagi

Good asparagus stands straight; the overlapping leaves that form its crown are packed tight. Asparagus will stay fresh for several days if you keep the stalks moist. Look for a jar that can accommodate the whole bunch, put a crumpled paper towel on the bottom, and pour water about an inch high over it. Moisten another sheet of paper towel, wrap it around the asparagus bunch, and stand the bunch upright inside the jar. Refrigerate for up to a week before prepping and cooking.

One of the most useful things I can say to someone who will cook this glorious vegetable is that if you are going to eat it on its own, and not cut up as an ingredient for a sauce, a frittata, or a risotto, you want the thickest stalks you can get. The sweetest, juiciest part of an asparagus is in its stalk; the thicker the stalk the more of that sweet, pale green flesh there is. To make use of it, you must pare away the tough dark green rind that sheathes the stalk. The broader the stalk the easier it is to work the peeler around it. There is no question that you must peel it. If you don't, you will end up discarding better than half of what is good to eat in an asparagus.

Before peeling, slice off a thin disk from the stalk's bottom. If the bottom is moist and fresh, a half inch may be sufficient, but if it is dry and woody, take off more. Working from the bottom of the stalk and moving upward, use a vegetable peeler with a swiveling blade to remove several layers of the dark skin until the pale core is exposed.

The tastiest thing you can do with asparagus is to gratinée it. I first blanch it for about a minute in boiling salted water, then I lay it flat in a baking dish dotted with butter and covered with a liberal grating of Parmesan cheese. I bake it in a 450° oven until a brown crust forms on top. If I feel very self-indulgent, I serve it with a fried egg on top. If I were to blanch it a little longer, I would drain it and serve it cold or still warm as a side dish, seasoned with salt, red wine vinegar, olive oil, and a droplet or two of balsamic vinegar.

Thin asparagus is what you want when you are cutting it up for a pasta sauce, perhaps one with cream and prosciutto, or adding it to a vegetable soup, or using in a risotto. You can then discard most of the stalk, which is too thin to peel and too tough to chew.

White asparagus is not a different variety; it is the same plant that has been denied access to chlorophyll-producing light by keeping it covered with soil or mulch while it grows. It is a culinary curiosity, not as sweet as green asparagus. I never buy it. If you do, you definitely must peel the stalks, because its skin is very tough.

Cranberry beans

BEANS

I Fagioli

SHELLING BEANS:
CRANBERRY, CANNELLINI, FAVA

I Fagioli da Sgranare: I Borlotti, I Cannellini, Le Fave

Shelling beans are those whose pods we don't eat. We may cook them freshly shelled or buy them dried to cook at a later time. Of the varieties of shelling beans I have tasted, borlotti and cannellini surpass all others in taste and texture. They both excel in any dish in which beans have a presence. Borlotti are earthy and meaty; cannellini are sweet, creamy, and delicately nutty. Borlotti triumph in the Veneto's *pasta e fagioli*, cannellini in the iconic Tuscan soup *la ribollita*.

Cranberry Beans/Borlotti

For Italian cooks in the north, borlotti are the default beans, matchless for *pasta e fagioli*, frequently part of a lamb stew or with other braised meats, sometimes paired with fresh shellfish, enjoyed in risotto or in a pasta sauce, but never more satisfying than when served alone, spilled still warm from the pot onto the plate, glistening with olive oil and speckled with black pepper, their dense, chestnut-like flesh accompanied by thick slices of soft country bread.

From late summer into deep autumn, the most striking sight in a produce market is a binful of fresh cranberry bean pods, pale yellow with flaming pink streaks. The beans within are white and marbled by pink markings that last only as long as they are raw, because they turn brown during cooking. Select pods that are firm, intact, and whose colors are bright. Reject any that are blackened or limp or show any sign of mold. I prefer to shell them immediately after bringing them home, because the pods do not stay fresh long in the refrigerator and take up a lot of space besides. Keep the shelled beans for up to a week in a tightly sealed plastic bag in the refrigerator's vegetable drawer.

When they are fresh, I like to cook borlotti in olive oil with onions and a pork bone of some kind or a piece of guanciale. If they are dried, I first soak them overnight, adding a pinch of salt to the water. The following morning I retrieve the reconstituted beans, strain the soaking water, and put the beans with their strained water, a few peeled garlic cloves, a bunch of fresh sage, and olive oil in a saucepan, with sufficient liquid to cover them by one and a half to two inches. After a very brief but lively initial boil, I add a tiny pinch of salt, turn the heat all the way down to a gentle simmer, then cook until tender, about two hours. You can also cook them for six hours or more in a slow cooker, the one job that contraption does best.

Dried beans will last a long time in the pantry if they are kept in a tightly closed glass or steel container, but they don't improve with age. At the end of a year there is a marked loss of flavor and texture. I keep vacuum-packed beans in the refrigerator and try to use them within six months of their harvest.

Should they ever come your way, do not pass up Italy's mountain-grown borlotti. They come from the northeastern-most corner of the country, grown in the foothills of the Alps at 1,800 feet above sea level. They are known and certified as fagioli di Lamon, the name of the township where they are produced. Fagioli di Lamon have thin skin and extraordinarily creamy flesh. Should you be visiting Venice, buy a pound or two of dried Lamon beans at Mascari's store in the market to cook when you are back home.

Cannellini

If you find yourself at a trattoria in the Tuscan countryside and the waiter suggests an appetizer of *fagioli sgranati*, what he will bring is a plate of warm cannellini, transparently tinged with the yellow-green of the olive oil in which they were cooked and with which they have just now been dressed. They're cannellini to the rest of the world, but for Tuscans the generic Italian word for beans, *fagioli*, is specific enough. What other kinds could matter?

There is a small, hilly area northwest of Florence called

Fava beans

Sorana, near the town of Pescia, in whose soil and climate cannellini beans achieve perfection. The skin of Sorana's cannellini is almost impalpable, enclosing creamy flesh unique in its nutty delicacy. The zone, no more than twenty-five acres, is as precious to the world of beans as the vineyards of Burgundy's Domaine de la Romanée-Conti are to the world of wine. The cannellini grown there are legally certified and protected by the appellation fagioli di Sorana.

Soak and cook dried cannellini beans, as well as other dried beans, by the method I described for borlotti.

Fava Beans

I love all food—meat, fish, cheese, grains, fruit—but where I have found the most profound and varied flavors has been in vegetables. If I were to rate a cuisine by what it does with its vegetables, by how simple are the preparations, how clear the tastes, lively and endearing like nothing else coming to the table, if those were the criteria on which to base my judgment, I'd have to give the prize to the cooking of the lower half of the Italian peninsula. Many of those dishes benefit from the presence of fava beans, the sequence and complexity of whose flavors are theirs alone, the wrinkled texture, the bristly earthiness of the skin, then the smoothness and suavity of the bean within it.

Fava beans need to be fresh for the best expression of their flavor and texture, but they can be either young or mature.

If they are very young, the size of a pinky's nail, enjoy them raw, with their skin on, the most flavorful part of the fava. Moisten with olive oil and serve with slivers of Parmigiano-Reggiano. If they are mature, the size of the first phalanx of a thumb, the raw skin will be chewy and bitter and should be eliminated by blanching the beans. Drop them into a pan of boiling water for one minute, drain, let them cool a moment, then, using the sharp tip of a paring knife, slit the narrow seam at the top of each bean, and squeeze the skin off. Sprinkle with a pinch of salt and serve with slivers of a mature pecorino, preferably not the salty romano. A six-month-old cheese from Tuscany, Corsica, or Spain is what I would choose. Drizzle olive oil over all and top with two or three fresh grindings of black pepper.

In the spring, Rome gives us *fave al guanciale*, fava beans cooked, with their skins on, in olive oil together with cured hog jowl. In Rome again, the taste of spring comes to a complete summation in the three vegetables of *la vignarola*, a dish that combines the earliest peas, the youngest fresh fava beans, and the first artichokes. Sicily has a nearly identical version called *la frittedda*. In Liguria—the Italian Riviera— fresh, small fava beans display their sweetest side when made into soup with romaine lettuce.

Fava's soft, velvety pod is as fuzzy to the touch as the beans inside it are smooth. The pods of fresh fava should have no dark pockmarks, no moldy spots, no limpness. Test one by holding it at each end and twisting it open. It should come apart crisply. Use the same method at home to shell them. The pods have no culinary value; discard them after shelling.

There are also dried fava beans, which must be soaked before they are cooked. Their flavor is simple, but intense. The most devastatingly delicious thing you can do with dried fava beans is the Apulian dish in which the cooked beans are pureed through a food mill or potato masher, then beaten, in the upper half of a double boiler, into milk-soaked bread and olive oil. Separately, sauté blanched rapini in olive oil and garlic, then combine on a plate with the fava bean purée.

CHICKPEAS, *CICERCHIA*, LENTILS

Ceci, Cicerchia, Lenticchie

To soak or not to soak, canned or dried, these are questions that may have different answers. When it comes to borlotti and cannellini, I find that recently harvested dried beans have better flavor and texture than the canned, therefore I am obliged to soak them many hours, usually overnight, before cooking. For several years, I used dried chickpeas that I soaked and cooked as I continue to do beans. Chickpeas, however, take a long time to cook evenly and fully, and the results are inconsistent. Canned chickpeas packed under the Goya Premium label are completely satisfactory, and I no longer struggle to soak and cook dried ones. There are so many uses for chickpeas—in soups; in a pasta sauce; sautéed in olive oil, garlic, and chili pepper with a green vegetable such as rapini; with braised meats, especially a lamb stew— that I buy a case at a time online directly from the company. Opening a can of high-quality chickpeas is such an easy, lazy way to complete a delicious salad. My own favorite is the simplest one: a tender lettuce such as Boston, chickpeas warmed briefly in a saucepan with a little water and drained, tossed with sea salt, red wine vinegar, olive oil, and a fresh grinding of black pepper. I may be the only person who skins the chickpeas after draining them, but it really does produce a pleasanter taste.

Chickpeas have been around a long time, but the origin of *cicerchia*, a similar pulse, is even older. Smaller than chickpeas, it has a more rustic flavor. *Cicerchia* doesn't come in a can that I know of. It must be soaked a minimum of eight hours, during which the water should be changed once or twice, and cooked at a simmer in fresh water. It is most satisfying in a country-style soup with vegetables and a couple of tomatoes.

The general opinion about lentils is that they don't need soaking. I have a different opinion. If you don't soak them, they absorb too much fluid from a soup or from other liquid cooking mediums, which dilutes some of their flavor. I don't soak them overnight; two hours are sufficient.

Some lentils are described as having zero tannins. Theirs

is a thin coat on a small seed. They cook quickly, their color stays bright, and they do not "muddy" the water. These may be desirable features, but their taste does not surpass, or sometimes even match that of other lentils. My favorite lentils are the tiny ones from the Colfiorito plateau in Umbria.

Beets

BEETS

Le Rape Rosse

There may be no point in telling you about the beets I used to buy at the Rialto market in Venice, but I want to tell you anyway. They are very small, so small that one of my editors who was visiting thought they were radishes. They are pink, very pale, and sometimes nearly white. Venetians, who have their own names for everything, call them *erbette*—"small grasses"—which other Italians find mystifying. What is even more mystifying about *erbette* is how something as low on the social scale as a beet can have such an enchanting taste, divinely sweet and delicate.

Beets have a long shelf life, but that is no reason to be less than selective when buying them. The first thing to look at is the leafy top. It must not be limp; it should spring healthily from the root and be colored a vivid green. If it is fresh you can assume that the root it's attached to will be equally so. The tops, moreover, make an excellent cooking green, nearly as sweet as spinach when fresh. The beet itself also deserves a look. Pass up any whose skin is damaged or wrinkled.

You can keep beets loose in the vegetable drawer of the refrigerator for a week or more, but if the tops are fresh enough to cook, detach them right away, cutting them about an inch above the beet's bulb. Separate the red stalks from the green leaves, but do not discard them, because they are also good to eat. Put the stalks first in boiling salted water. When they have boiled three to four minutes, put in the leaves, which will cook very quickly after coming to a boil. I serve the stalks and leaves separately so that one may take as much of either as one may like. I like them best of all dressed with salt, lemon juice, and olive oil.

Cook the beets either by boiling them or roasting them, wrapped in foil, in a 400° oven. They are likely to be a little sweeter when roasted, but I prefer to boil them on top of the stove, where I can more easily take an occasional look at them. Whichever method you choose, they will take a long time to become tender, how long is difficult to predict. Depending on their size and the specific qualities of individual beets, they may take from one and a half hours to three hours or more. They are done when a fork or other sharply pointed implement pierces them easily. Drain them. It seems a pity to discard the intensely red liquid, but there is no use for it that I have found. Rinse the beets in cold water to make them more comfortable to hold, and use a paring knife to peel them. If you don't want to stain your fingers, use gloves. I dress sliced beets in the same manner as I do the leaves, except that for beets I prefer red wine vinegar to lemon juice.

CHIOGGIA BEETS

For me, red beets are the most satisfying in taste and hue, but beets do come in other colors: orange-gold, turnip-white, purple, and with internal concentric fuchsia candy stripes. The latter are known as Chioggia beets after the town south of Venice where they were developed. Candy-striped beets have two winning features. They are sweeter than the red, for some almost too mild-tasting, and they don't dye their cooking water with a color hard to eradicate should it spill on your clothes. The pretty concentric stripes fade in cooking. It is often suggested to add lemon juice or vinegar to the water to make the stripes more visible, but I don't find that it alters the outcome. If it's the stripes you are after, serve the beets raw, sliced very thin, possibly with a mandoline. All beets call for a generous dose of vinegar in their seasoning, and Chioggia beets even more than the conventional red.

BROCCOLI

Il Broccolo a Testa

When I see broccoli florets bagged for sale at the store, I wonder: What happened to the stems? The flavorful, juicy stem is every bit as good as asparagus, but cooks often discard it, first because they don't know how delicious it is, and second because they won't be bothered to peel away the hard, dark rind. It's a pity, because the meaty, pale flesh at broccoli's core may well be more enjoyable than the cabbagey florets. Even children might like it.

When buying broccoli, examine the stem. It should have an overall fresh look, and the exposed center of its cut end should be a pale, moist-looking green. Avoid exceptionally thick stems, because they are overgrown and stringy. The head of florets must be tightly packed and a bright, solid green color. Any yellowing and opening up of the head are signs of age. Fresh broccoli will keep up to five days in an open plastic bag in the refrigerator's vegetable drawer.

To prepare a stem for cooking, detach it from the head and use a vegetable peeler with a swiveling blade to pare away all of the dark, tough rind that surrounds it, thus exposing the pale, tender core. If you find any strings after it's cooked, it means either that the broccoli was old or that you didn't peel it down enough.

To my taste, the best thing you can do with very fresh broccoli is to cook it in liberally salted boiling water. Drop in the well-trimmed stems first, cook for about three to four minutes, then put in the florets, their tops facing up, and cook for an additional four minutes. Drain, sprinkle it with crunchy sea salt and either a fine red wine vinegar or lemon juice, toss, and anoint with a good, fruity olive oil. Eat it while still warm, if possible.

Other excellent employments for broccoli are baked under a thick cover of grated Parmesan cheese, sautéed with garlic and olive oil, in a vegetable soup, or as a pasta sauce. If choosing to make pasta sauce, briefly blanch the broccoli, chop it coarsely, and sauté it in olive oil with garlic, chili pepper, and mashed anchovies.

The stems are also very nice raw. After peeling them, cut them lengthwise into two or more pieces and season with salt and olive oil. I have had them in Asian restaurants served with sesame oil, and I loved them.

Savoy cabbage

CABBAGES

I Cavoli

SAVOY CABBAGE, LA VERZA

The pleasure of cooking with Savoy cabbage is such that in my cookbooks I had difficulty limiting myself to just a few examples of its flexibility. My editor snapped, "What are all these recipes? Did the market have a sale on Savoy cabbage?" Where does one stop? Rollups with pork and rice? A salad with cannellini beans? Frittata with leeks? Soup with chickpeas? Pasta sauce with sausages? Stuffed together with ground meat in ravioli? In risotto with cranberry beans or pork ribs? In Valtellina's pizzoccheri pasta? Smothered Venetian style? With meatballs? Cut up with Swiss chard and rapini and sautéed in garlic and olive oil? I could have gone on, and indeed I did. Among leafy cabbages, this native of Piedmont has no competition.

Unlike tightly packed green cabbage, which is not popular with Italians, the beautiful, frilly, ribbed outer leaves of Savoy cabbage are loose and open. The center of the head should feel firm, however. The colors range from very deep to light green. The flavor of the lighter green is better developed, but both are good. Savoy does not keep as long as ordinary cabbage; do not let it exceed ten days in the refrigerator. Do not wash it before refrigerating it. If you cannot use the whole head at once, cut off what you need and store the remainder in a loose plastic bag.

GREEN CABBAGE, IL CAVOLO CAPPUCCIO

Had Victor not mistakenly picked up a green cabbage in the market instead of the Savoy cabbage I had sent him for, I probably never would have cooked one. At home, the only cabbages my mother used were the infinitely versatile Savoy and the sweet red cabbage. The frugal cooks of Venice, however, where we lived for many years, make liberal use of the humble pale green cabbage, shredding it fine and cooking it over the stove in olive oil, a little bit of red wine vinegar, and its own odorous vapors. It's a method called *sofegao*—"smothered"—in the local dialect. I liked the taste so well that I put it in one of my cookbooks.

Green or white cabbage is almost never absent from the market bins, and when there is no Savoy, I use it if I am making a vegetable soup. I can never have too many vegetables in my minestrone; Victor once counted eighteen. I may even put it alongside pork in a stew, or with chicken in a fricassee.

RED CABBAGE, IL CAVOLO ROSSO

Red cabbage I love. It is sweet and gentle and does delicious, dark things when it is shredded fine and braised with small meats, such as chicken, rabbit, or lamb.

Select cabbage heads by their solidity and the compactness and crispness of their leaves. Greengrocers keep their cabbages looking fresh by stripping away the outer leaves when they begin to wilt. The inner leaves are always paler, therefore the darker the outside leaves are, the fresher the cabbage is and the tastier it will be. Another clue to its freshness is the stem, which should not show cracks or appear parched. If taste and freshness matter, do not buy shredded cabbage. If the head is intact, it will keep quite well for at least a week and a half refrigerated inside an open plastic bag.

CARROTS

Le Carote

Carrots are the least problematic vegetable to buy, store, prep, and cook, and no other can produce a more universally endearing flavor. A generous handful of chopped carrots, slowly sautéed, provides the sweet foundation of a Bolognese sauce or a base on which to rest the step-by-step assemblage of a classic minestrone's many vegetables. When serving them entirely on their own, I am fond of slicing them into thin rounds and braising them very slowly in butter in a broad skillet with just enough water, replenished tablespoon by tablespoon, to keep the cooking going without ever turning them until they become wrinkled and colored a dark orange-brown. With slow and patient cooking, the intensity of flavor that the humble root can release is a revelation. The one cooking method that does nothing for carrots, or for anyone eating them, is boiling or steaming. Water can be most unkind to carrots.

Buy carrots that are brightly colored; smooth of skin; firm, not limp; and sound, not cracked. I prefer medium-size carrots to the overly large, which are doughy and not as sweet. If the tops are still on, you can easily judge their freshness. You may want to use the tops. I do not, but even if you do, cut them off before stowing the carrots in the refrigerator; otherwise they will drain away moisture from the root. Store carrots in a plastic bag in the refrigerator's vegetable drawer, where they will keep for as long as two weeks.

Before using the carrots, rinse them in cold water, cut off a thin disk from the stem end, and peel them using a vegetable peeler with a swiveling blade. I peel even small carrots—I don't mean miniatures—because otherwise they will have a slightly musty taste of earth.

CAULIFLOWER

Il Cavolfiore

There are two sides to cauliflower's profile, one brash, the other mild. Each modifies the other and rounds its appeal. Boiled and served still warm in the Italian manner, seasoned with salt, red wine vinegar, and excellent olive oil, cauliflower can be extraordinarily soothing. Or it can be feisty in a pasta sauce with garlic, olive oil, anchovies, and chili pepper. Or it acquires a polished manner when blanched and baked with béchamel and bits of ham. If there is a context that I find uncongenial to cauliflower, it is with seafood, although there are chefs who think otherwise. Raw it is definitely unpleasant; should it land on my plate next to a chop or some shrimp or anything else, I would push it to a far side.

However I choose to cook it, I always blanch it first to soften it. To my taste, and to the characteristic taste of Italian cooking, there is nothing enjoyable about an unyielding crunch in vegetables, and in cauliflower it would be the least agreeable of all. To prepare cauliflower for cooking, detach the leaves and pare away the very bottom of the base. The head can be cooked whole or, to save time, it can be halved or quartered. Do not discard the core, which has good flavor if cooked until tender.

Buy cauliflower whose head of tightly packed florets is unblemished, completely free of dark spots. A small head will taste sweeter and cook faster than a large one. Cauliflower doesn't keep very long, and it should be tightly wrapped in plastic wrap before refrigerating. Cook it within three or four days.

Romanesco or Broccoflower

It is a cauliflower of Roman origin whose beautiful green head is cone-shaped with many tight little pyramidal floret clusters. It is cooked like regular cauliflower. The green color fades when cooked, but the taste is sweeter than that of other cauliflowers. One may also cook its tender leaves.

CELERY

Il Sedano

Should you decide to make a Bolognese sauce or a full-scale minestrone or any of scores of dishes that require a vegetable *soffritto*—a base of sautéed onion and minced carrot—you must absolutely have celery on hand. It keeps a long while, so there is no reason not to buy it before you need to use it. The question you might have is whether to get the pre-cut packaged ribs or a whole celery. The packaged celery takes less room, but a whole celery is a better choice. It is fresher, as you can judge from the condition of the leaves, which must be bright green and erect. The leaves, moreover, are very useful cooked in a braise or in any dish where you need a stronger celery aroma than the ribs alone can provide. When possible, choose celery whose green color is pale rather than dark, because it is sweeter.

Whenever I bought celery at the market in Italy, the stall keeper handed it to me wrapped in butcher paper. I stored it in the vegetable compartment of my refrigerator still wrapped in that paper and placed loosely inside a plastic bag. It stayed fresh for close to a month. In Florida, where we now live, I wrap a whole celery in paper towels and refrigerate it inside a plastic bag. To keep its moisture from leaking to the base and the leaves, I trim away some of the base and cut off the leaves, keeping these in a separate airtight bag.

Peel away as many of the strings as you can, particularly from the thick outer ribs, using a vegetable peeler with a swiveling blade. Work up from the bottom.

Celery's role in cooking is usually a secondary one, but it can also emerge on its own, as it does in one of my family's favorite dishes. When you have pulled away all the strings, cut the ribs into two or three pieces, peel some potatoes and cut them into wedges, put both celery and potatoes in a saucepan with salt, olive oil, and lemon juice, cover the pan, and cook over gentle heat until the potatoes and celery are tender. Look into the pan from time to time, turning its contents and, if necessary to keep them from sticking to the bottom, add a little bit of water. Serve as soon as done.

Radicchio Tardivo, Radicchio di Chioggia,
Radicchio di Treviso

THE CHICORY FAMILY

Le Cicorie

RADICCHIO, ENDIVE, ESCAROLE, PUNTARELLE, ASPARAGUS CHICORY, SUGARLOAF, DANDELION, FRISÉE

*Il Radicchio, La Belga, La Scarola, Le Puntarelle,
La Catalogna, Il Radicchio di Milano, Il Dente di Leone,
L'Insalatina Riccia*

In the vegetable world, there is no feistier family than the chicories. Raw they can be defiantly crisp; cooking will soften the crispness while stirring the palate with bitter accents that can be either understated or bold, but never easy to ignore.

Radicchio chicories constitute the main branch of the family. The most familiar one to American cooks is the dark red variety known as radicchio di Chioggia, named after the town near Venice where it originated. White-ribbed leaves cling tightly to a firm cabbage-like head. Before the grocer pulls off any wilting and discolored outer leaves, the head is the size of a large grapefruit. When it becomes the size of a large orange, it's a sign that some of its leaves have been removed, and it is no longer quite fresh. Chioggia is better raw in a salad, when one can enjoy its lively crunch and blunted tang of bitterness, which in cooking turns sharp. In one of my favorite salads, I shred radicchio leaves with a knife, slice some onion very thin, and toss everything with warm cannellini beans, seasoning the salad very simply with sea salt, red wine vinegar, and olive oil. For another of my radicchio salads, I tear the leaves into irregular pieces, rub a few crusts of bread with garlic, and toss both together with the usual insuperable dressing of salt, red wine vinegar, and olive oil. No, no balsamic.

The torpedo-shaped radicchio di Treviso, which is less bitter than the Chioggia, is a better choice for cooking, shredded and sautéed with pancetta or split in half and baked with olive oil. Its romaine-like leaves are excellent in salads.

When the radicchio di Treviso plant is subjected to a laborious cultivation method forcing the direction of its growth and shielding it from sunlight, it develops into the spectacular end-of-season vegetable known as radicchio tardivo, late-harvest radicchio. The technique of forced growth pares down its leaves to just a frilly, fiery red fringe bordering thick, glossy, white ribs that curl, flamelike, upward and inward from an elongated root. Radicchio tardivo is extravagantly good in salads—no other green matches it—but its destiny is in cooking. Grilled tardivo, risotto with tardivo, and fettuccine with tardivo and bacon are some of the dishes that showcase the glorious flavors of this noble vegetable.

The belle of the radicchio clan is radicchio di Castelfranco. Its soft leaves, the color of corn and cream speckled with lavender red, unfold like flower petals around a tender head. Castelfranco pairs well with cheese and makes an admirable contribution to salads.

Store all radicchio varieties in loose plastic bags in the refrigerator's vegetable drawer, and expect to use them within a week.

Belgian endive is a lovely, small chicory grown by a method similar to that used with radicchio tardivo. It is kept in the dark to turn the color of the leaves, tapering tightly along the head, into a delicate ivory white with pale yellow tips. When I use Belgian endive in a mixed greens salad, I cut it across into rounds. It is ravishingly good baked, and the best method is also the simplest. Split each head in two lengthwise, sprinkle with salt and pepper, coat it liberally with olive oil, and bake until it is very soft and its edges are lightly browned. Chicory bitterness subsides after this treatment. Belgian endive is sometimes crossed with radicchio di Treviso to stain it red. It is pretty if raw, but it turns white when cooked. Choose medium to large heads that are full and firm with leaves of a glossy ivory color. When the endive is no longer fresh, the leaves become duller and darker, and a rusty tint may appear at the base. Store each head wrapped in a paper towel in a plastic bag in the vegetable drawer of the refrigerator. They will stay in good shape for about ten days.

Curly endive is not a variety of Belgian endive, but the larger form of frisée, described on page 45. A more interesting chicory is escarole, *scarola* in Italian, a vegetable with broad, wavy, light green leaves forming a soft head whose center is composed of a thicket of small, pale leaves. When it is grown shielded from sunlight, some of the green in the leaves turns to white. Its taste is almondy, not bitter like radicchio. It has a great many uses in the kitchen, aside from being an excellent salad vegetable. It can be braised or sautéed in olive oil, it is sometimes boiled and dressed with lemon juice and olive oil, and it finds its way into the filling of rustic pies and inside rolled-up meats and meatballs. You can store a whole head of escarole for four or five days in the refrigerator, wrapped tightly in a large plastic bag.

Another fascinating chicory is the tall asparagus chicory, *catalogna* in Italian. A crown of long, slender dark green leaves cradles within it a mass of white, twisted spears called *puntarelle*, whose tips resemble those of asparagus. One removes the spears, which are hollow, and slices them lengthwise into thin strips one-quarter-inch wide. They are soaked for about an hour in a bowl of ice water wherein they curl up. You dry them and sauce them with a mixture of salt, vinegar, garlic, minced anchovies, ground black pepper, and olive oil. It becomes a salad that is incomparably refreshing, crunchy and tasty. When *puntarelle* are not available, you can apply the same treatment to the leaves of Belgian endive.

Sugarloaf chicory, known in Italy as radicchio di Milano, is a green radicchio that resembles a head of romaine lettuce. The pale core is mild in flavor and it is very crisp, delightful in salads.

Dandelion, *dente di leone*, and sometimes *cicorino*, in Italian, may be either cultivated or foraged. The stem is hard and as much of it as possible should be trimmed away. It can be served, shredded fine, in a salad of small mixed greens or added to a vegetable soup. Refrigerate wrapped in a paper towel inside a large resealable plastic bag. It can stay fresh up to a week.

A sweeter tasting, very small cultivated radicchio called *radicchietto* in Italian is an essential part of a *misticanza*, the mix of tiny, fresh salad greens better known here as mesclun.

Frisée, the smaller edition of curly endive, is purely a salad chicory that contributes its frilly, gently bitter, yellowish-green leaves to a *misticanza*. It adds variety to a mix but becomes tedious if served only on its own. Keep it inside a loose plastic bag in the refrigerator's vegetable drawer, where it should stay fresh for a week.

CUCUMBERS

I Cetrioli

When I was very young, the fragrance of the first freshly sliced cucumber of the summer was my signal that for the following few weeks I could swim, play volleyball on the beach, race around town on a bicycle with my friends, and consume a daily salad of tomatoes, raw onion, and sliced cucumber. It was the very smell and taste of the Italian summers of my youth. Cucumbers have long since become available every day of the year, losing in the process most of their stirring seasonal flavor.

I've heard about many varieties of cucumbers, but I usually find only three: The basic ones that most people buy are thick, smooth-skinned, and glossy; there are elongated dark green cucumbers called English or Continental that are usually tightly wrapped in plastic; there are short, gnarled ones sometimes labeled Kirbies. The first two are for slicing. The thick, smooth-skinned cucumber is often waxed and I always peel it. If you need to see whether it has more seeds than you'd like, split it in half along its length before slicing it to expose the seed-laden core. If it is too thick with seeds for you, use a teaspoon to scoop them out. The skinny, plastic-wrapped cucumber does not need peeling. It has very few seeds, a pleasant flavor, and a subdued, hardly perceptible aroma. The Kirbies are the ones that people buy for pickling. I don't do that, but I buy them to eat raw because I like their compact flesh and recognizable cucumber flavor. They don't need peeling.

Choose your cucumbers by their firmness. They must not have a single soft spot. It is desirable for the smooth, glossy variety to have a narrow streak of yellow—a yellow belly—a sign of ripeness. I keep an unwashed whole cucumber for no more than a week in the refrigerator, wrapped in a paper towel and stowed in a loose plastic bag. If cut in half but unwashed, I wrap it tightly in plastic wrap and refrigerate it for two or three days. If sliced, I close the slices in a resealable plastic bag and keep them in the vegetable drawer of the fridge for two days.

Cucumber performs its finest role when sliced in a salad with ripe summer tomatoes and raw onion slices. Season it with coarse sea salt; a fresh squeeze of lemon juice or red wine vinegar, but not balsamic; and excellent olive oil. Salt causes cucumber, which is nearly all water, to weep copiously. To prevent it from making the salad soggy, toss the cucumber slices with salt and a few drops of lemon juice in a separate dish. When the salad is ready for the table, retrieve the cucumber slices with a slotted spoon, leaving behind the liquid they have shed, and combine them with the already dressed tomato and onion. My mother used to add basil, my mother-in-law parsley. If the tomato is what it ought to be, it can manage without such herbal scents.

I like cucumber with smoked salmon. Whichever kind I am having, I peel it because the skin's bitterness doesn't flatter the salmon. I cut it in four or more lengthwise sections, depending on its girth. If it is a long cucumber, I also cut it across in half.

I sometimes use a scooped-out half cucumber as the recipient of a mousse of prosciutto and minced pickles or of a whip of tuna, butter, and anchovies or just of good anchovies mashed with unsalted butter. Serve it with drinks or at table.

I also dice peeled, seeded cucumber and mix it, with a Middle Eastern accent, into the soft flesh of a baked eggplant.

EGGPLANT

Le Melanzane

The eggplants you buy at a farmers' market are usually quite fresh, whereas the ones from the supermarket are likely to have experienced a longer interval between harvest and the move into the store's vegetable bin. There is one accurate clue to freshness. Look at the little green cap by which the eggplant was attached to the plant. The brighter green that cap, the fresher the eggplant. When it has been around a long while, the cap turns brown, dull, and dusty-looking. Examine the skin; it should be glossy, taut, and completely smooth. Squeeze the eggplant gently. It must not feel spongy; it should spring back firmly from your touch. When held in the hand, it ought to feel light; if it is heavy in the hand it could be weighed down by too many seeds.

All eggplants, whatever their color, which may be purple, pale lavender, striped, or ivory white, and whatever their shape, which may be thick and bulbous, round, or skinny and short or skinny and long, yield flesh that is creamy and sweet when the vegetable is baked whole or sliced and fried. It is less sweet, and even bitter sometimes, when cut into chunks and sautéed. In this instance, you may first purge the eggplant of bitter juices by cutting it open and placing it along the sides of a colander, dusting it with kosher salt, and allowing the issuing juice to drain away over thirty or forty minutes.

If frying eggplant slices for a parmigiana or a Sicilian pasta sauce, it may be prudent to follow the purging method, salting them ahead of time and allowing possibly bitter juices to drain away. Pat the slices dry and dredge them in flour before frying.

One type of eggplant that is guaranteed to be sweet is the Asian variety, long and skinny. White or striped eggplants also have very good flavor, but their skins are tougher, and you should peel them.

Grilled eggplant slices may sound good in a menu and add to the visual appeal of a plate, but they do nothing for taste. If you want to grill an eggplant, halve it lengthwise, use the point of a sharp knife to crosshatch the flesh, dust it with salt, sprinkle lightly with lemon juice, and moisten the flesh with olive oil, forcing some of it into the crosshatched cracks. Grill it skin side down until it feels very soft when poked with a fork.

If I have a large, bulbous eggplant, I'll bake it whole in a 400° oven for about forty-five minutes, turning it once, until it collapses. Melt a little butter in a small skillet and toast a handful of pine nuts, allowing them to darken. Scoop the very soft flesh out of the eggplant, add salt, drops of lemon juice, olive oil, and the toasted pine nuts; and mix it all up.

FENNEL

Il Finocchio

In earlier, more wicked days of the wine business in Florence, when merchants poured samples of the new vintage for their customers, they first served them nibbles of sliced *finocchio*, believing that the taste of licorice on the palate would soften the edges of rough young wine. The practice led to the coinage of a verb, *infinocchiare*, which means to hoodwink.

Finocchio, the icon of Italian vegetables, has many other more respectable and appetizing uses. Without doubt, most of it is consumed raw, either sliced very thin horizontally or cut into wedges. If sliced, fennel often finds its way into a mixed salad, but it is most refreshing served alone, seasoned with salt, a drop of vinegar or lemon juice to dissolve the salt, black pepper ground fresh from a mill, and fruity olive oil.

This white bulb, which can be as hard and large as a boxer's fist, holds luscious reserves of aromatic juices that it releases only when it is cooked by one of the methods in the classic Italian trilogy of vegetable cookery, braised or fried or baked. In each instance it must first be cut into quarter-inch slices, cutting the bulb straight down from the top. To braise, cook the fennel slices with olive oil and barely enough water to cover them in a deep skillet or open sauce-

Fennel

pan for about thirty minutes, until they are tender at the pricking of a fork.

To fry the slices, first blanch them briefly in salted boiling water, drain, and let them cool down. Dip in beaten egg, then coat with bread crumbs. Fry in very hot vegetable oil, turning them once, until they form a crisp, golden-brown crust on each side. Sprinkle with salt and serve while still hot.

To bake, slice and blanch the fennel, arrange the slices in a baking dish, dot with butter, blanket with Parmesan grated at that moment, and cook in a preheated 450° oven until a golden crust forms on top.

You may see fennel in the market all year, but it is best from December to early spring. The bulbs have two shapes: round and squat or flat and elongated. Italian cooks refer to the stockier shape as the male and the flat, tapered shape as the female. The male is juicier and sweeter and certainly better to eat raw. It would be better in cooked dishes as well, but there the female, if fresh, can also be satisfactory. Sometimes the bulb is small, light in weight, and very flat. It was harvested too soon and did not have time to develop. Don't bother with it; leave it in the store.

Look for fennel with its tops on, because bright, unwilted leaves are a sign of freshness. You will cut off the tops before you use the bulbs. If you like their aroma, you may find use for the fragrance of the leaves in soups and stews. The bulb itself should feel heavy for its size, and its thick outer leaves should be intact, bearing no gashes or bruises. If you are not cooking it immediately, cut off the leaves and store the fennel's bulb in an open plastic bag in the vegetable drawer for up to a week or even ten days, depending on its freshness. When preparing fennel for a salad or for cooking, wash it on the outside under cold running water, then wash it again after cutting it.

GARLIC

L'Aglio

The garlic population is divided into hardnecks and soft-necks. Which neck to buy, assuming you have a choice? It depends on whether you store garlic for a few weeks or a few months, whether you are adept at peeling the cloves, whether you prefer large cloves to small. Most important, it is a decision about taste.

A hardneck garlic bulb is impaled on a long stem, known as a scape, which grows through the center of the bulb, emerging with considerable length beyond the bulb's top. Softneck garlic is spared penetration by a scape; hence, where the garlic head comes to a point, its "neck" remains soft.

The single great advantage of the softneck is that the skins can cling tightly to the top of the bulb, bestowing on it a long storage life by sealing in its moist juices. If stored well, soft-neck garlic will last in good condition for as long as a year, compared with approximately four months for hardnecks. Softnecks are what you find in the grocery store bin, grown either in China or California. They can be braided, either for kitchen decoration or for presentation as gifts. Softneck garlic has a large number of small to medium cloves tightly

Hardneck garlic

enclosed in their skin. Peeling requires varying degrees of pressure, applied by placing the flat side of a large knife over the clove and giving that side of the knife a sharp rap.

Hardneck garlic thrives in cool growing zones, although it can be cultivated in a mild climate by dedicated growers. The ones we find in farmers' markets, often tied by their necks in bunches, are likely to come from Canada. There exist hundreds of varieties that, when cooked, release marvelous aromas and flavors that softnecks cannot match. There are few cloves in a hardneck bulb, as few as eight, not more than twelve. They are large and lovely, those cloves, easy to peel, often requiring no pressure at all. I can usually lift and loosen the skin by gently poking the tip of my fingernail into it.

I buy hardneck garlic online, because so far no one brings it to the Sarasota markets. My favorite variety is called Georgian Fire. It usually has about six magnificent, burnished bulbs ready to slip out of their skin. The flavor is rich, harmonious, and warm. One of the best-known hardneck varieties is called Rocambole, from Canada. It is a beautiful garlic, with large, shiny cloves and deep, round flavor.

Prepare garlic for cooking with a view to the flavor you are after. For the mildest flavor, the kind that you want in a fine tomato sauce, use whole, peeled cloves. Cook them gently in olive oil, turning them from time to time, until they become colored a tawny gold. Do not ever let them burn, which is the flavor of crudely interpreted Italian cooking. For a slightly deeper flavor, crack the clove with the handle of a large knife or with a meat pounder. If you cut the peeled cloves into very thin slices you move one small step up in intensity. For the headiest garlic flavor and aroma, in rustic preparations where you are using chili pepper and mashed anchovies, chop the peeled cloves very fine. If I am caught critically short of time or feeling lazy, I drop the peeled cloves into the smaller bowl of a food processor while the blade is running. Do not heat up the oil before putting in the garlic. It may have become too hot, and the garlic might burn. I always put in the oil and garlic at the same time. It's the commonsensical and reliable way to do it. I apply the same principle to sautéing chopped onions. I usually do not use both onions and garlic, but if I do, after the onions have become lightly colored, I turn the heat down a bit and add the garlic.

There are some things I never do with garlic. I do not use a garlic press, which extracts too much pungency. I do not remove the green sprout. It is said to be bitter, but I have never used so much of it that it could make a discernible difference. I never mash salt into chopped garlic. That is a French technique, which makes the garlic moist and difficult to brown efficiently.

Select garlic heads that are plump, firm, and heavy for their size, their papery skins clinging tightly. Avoid those with dark or soft spots. Store garlic in a dry place. I find that having a couple of large, perforated, and lidded clay containers is a reliable way to keep garlic dry and well-ventilated. Humidity is its enemy. Do not refrigerate it. Do not experiment with keeping peeled cloves in olive oil. It is unnecessary and even dangerous. Do not buy peeled garlic in jars. Nothing compares to the taste of freshly peeled, healthy garlic cloves. Check the garlic in your containers periodically to verify that it is still in good, dry condition.

GREEN BEANS

I Fagiolini

Some people call them snap beans, and that is exactly what a fresh green bean should do when you bring its ends together between your thumb and forefinger: It should snap crisply in two. If it bends without snapping it has lain around too long. Another indication of freshness is at the end where the stem was attached to the plant. If there is still a piece of the stem on it and it is a bright green, the bean is fresh; if it is brown, the bean is old. The general appearance of a mound of green beans should be bright. The beans should be fairly uniform in size. If they are of various sizes, if they are dull-looking, if some are mottled, if they are cut and missing their ends, they have been carelessly harvested or are old or both. They are not worth cooking.

If they are fresh, it is best to cook them soon, or refrigerate in an open plastic bag for no more than two or three days. Before you cook them, rinse them thoroughly in cold water, then snap or cut off both ends. I used to do them one by one, but I no longer have that patience. I line them up on the counter, a dozen or so at a time, and chop off the ends.

Really good beans deserve the simplest of treatments. They should be cooked in salted boiling water until they are tender yet firm, but not crunchy. Crunchy beans are grassy in taste, and moreover, they are not enjoyable to chew. I time the cooking at seven minutes after the water I dropped them in has returned to a boil. A minute more is preferable to a minute less. Season the drained, warm beans with sea salt, red wine vinegar, and very good olive oil and have them with bread to sop up the oil.

In another favorite way to cook them, I slice a small onion very thin, sprinkle it lightly with salt, and cook it in olive oil with diced pancetta or guanciale and a pinch of red Italian chili pepper until it is golden and soft. I add tomatoes, either fresh, ripe Roma tomatoes peeled and cut up or canned, imported, genuine San Marzanos. I turn the tomatoes once or twice, then drop in the raw, trimmed beans and cook them at moderate heat for about an hour, occasionally turning them over.

HORSERADISH

Il Cren

Venetians like to forget that, for a brief time in their past, Austria was their master, but culinary mementos of those otherwise humiliating decades were welcomed to the Venetian table, where they survive today. One of them is horseradish. It has a couple of Italian names, *rafano* or *barbaforte*, but Venice continues to use the original German one, *cren*.

Horseradish is a thick root, available fresh in many American markets. It must be peeled, cut up, and grated so that it can be made into a sauce. The homemade version is infinitely more flavorful than anything you can buy, and it is extremely simple to make. The basic ingredient of the sauce, aside from the grated horseradish itself, is white wine vinegar, which stabilizes it. Also add a pinch or two of salt. Venetians and other cooks often put in a spoonful of sugar to round off the sharp horseradish bite. I prefer to use a tea-spoon or two of good balsamic vinegar. I also add olive oil to the mixture, because it gives it a silken texture as well as good flavor.

The food processor is an ideal tool for grating the horse-radish after you've peeled and chopped it. It creates a superbly uniform spread and spares you the tears as well as the effort that come with a hand grater. The fumes of grated fresh horseradish are seriously strong. Avert your head when you lift the food processor cover. Refrigerate the sauce in a tightly closed glass container. It should keep its potency for a month or longer. It is the ideal condiment for a *bollito misto*, the Italian assortment of boiled meats, and it adds a piquant, fragrant accent to a roast, a mixed grill or smoked fish, lunch meats, or hot dogs.

Choose horseradish root no thicker than one and a half inches because over that it begins to be fibrous. Look for a pale, fresh cream color. The root should feel solid, with no dark, spongy spots.

Lacinato kale

LACINATO KALE

Il Cavolo Nero

Some vegetables, like zucchini, say, or potatoes, seem endowed with ubiquity. They are an easy fit. Others thrive in a narrow culinary habitat, a small repertory of dishes that allow their temperament complete freedom of expression. The variety of kale known in Italian as *cavolo nero*, and here often labeled lacinato, needs a liquid medium for an uninhibited and enjoyable release of its earthy flavors, finding its most favorable opportunity in the Tuscan bread soup called *ribollita*, to whose alchemical twice-cooked fusion of vegetables and cannellini beans kale is indispensable.

The green-black, knobby, deckle-edged leaves of this unusual cabbage do not come together into a solid head. They are sold loose by weight. Choose firm, dark leaves with no discolorations or blemishes. If you are not using them the day you buy them, refrigerate them unwashed in an open plastic bag. They should keep at least a week. Before cooking, however, wash them thoroughly in several changes of cold water.

The stem at the center of the leaves is too tough to eat and must be removed. The neatest way to do it is to lay a leaf flat on a cutting board and run the sharp point of a paring knife along each side of the stem, separating the leaf in two halves without tearing them. Once you've liberated them from the stem, roll up each half leaf and slice it into ready-to-cook strips.

LEEKS

I Porri

Leeks enjoy a privileged place in my memories. When Victor and I married, we could afford a honeymoon of only one day, which we took in Sirmione, a resort on Lake Garda. It was winter, there were no tourists, only one or two commercial travelers, and we could indulge ourselves in imagining that the modest pensione where we stayed was open just for us. The food that was brought to our table in the small dining room tasted embracingly of good family fare. We still remember a robust soup of leeks and potatoes, a soup that I have been making since, for my husband and myself, in every year of the six decades that followed that night.

Leeks, looking like scallions with grossly enlarged bulbs, are invariably described as related to onions and garlic, but milder. Yes, they are milder, but they have scents and tastes that want to be admired for what they are, not because they are shyer than those of onions and garlic, but because they are subtle, distinctive, desirable, and irreplaceable. Leeks are magnificent, sweet braising vegetables on their own, cooked with either olive oil or butter, or braised with meats. The pork loin with leeks that I published in *Marcella's Italian Kitchen* has been a favorite meat dish for me and for many of my readers. Leeks are excellent with dark-fleshed fish such as bluefish and mackerel and fresh sardines. They are obligatory in a mixed vegetable soup. They make a gracious companion for cannellini in a bean soup. They dissolve creamily in a risotto. They elevate the fragrance of a meat broth when you add their tops, as well as the bulbs, to the other ingredients in the pot.

The leeks you buy must have bright green, firm, crisp leaves, the long white stalk must be intact, showing no bruises, and the bulb's bottom should be more flat than round. Leeks come small to very large, but exceptionally large leeks are the least desirable. When the bulb is much broader than one inch, it may have a fibrous center that you would need to discard.

To prep for cooking, begin by cutting off the roots and a thin slice from the base of the bulb. Detach the bulb and the white stalk, which are parts you will cook. Make a length-wise cut to strip away the first green outer leaves from the tops, which must be discarded, exposing a pale, whitish green core that you detach and add to the bulb and white stalk. Make one or two additional long cuts to strip away the remaining green portion of the leaves, exposing some more of the pale leek core that you will add to the parts you have already set aside for cooking.

In order to produce leeks whose stalks have more of the tender, edible white part, farmers pile up dirt over them to shield them from light during their growth. This means that there can be a considerable amount of soil in between the leek's layers that you must wash away thoroughly, both before and after prepping. After I have cut up a leek, I soak its parts in a basin of cold water, changing the water until there is no longer any soil settling to the bottom of the basin.

Unwashed leeks fresh from the market will keep in a loose plastic bag in the refrigerator for three to four days.

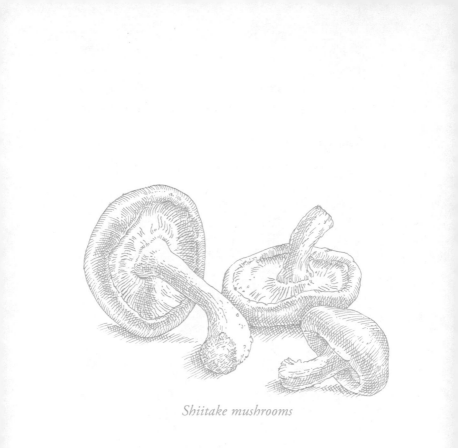

Shiitake mushrooms

MUSHROOMS

I Funghi

After a rain, thousands of different wild mushrooms raise their heads in the woods, but it is rare that any of them makes its way into our kitchens. Virtually every fresh mushroom we buy in America is cultivated and, with few exceptions, it is produced from a single variety that can be either white or brown. When immature, the white mushrooms are called button mushrooms, champignons, or simply small white mushrooms. The small brown ones are labeled either baby bella or cremini. When a baby bella matures, developing a large meaty cap, it is known as portobello.

The other variety of fresh mushroom that I often use because it merges well with Italian flavors is shiitake, which has been so successfully cultivated that it has become available everywhere. I shop where shiitakes are sold loose and choose the ones with the largest unblemished caps. They make a fleshy biteful, those caps, juicy and aromatic. I discard the stems, which are fibrous and too tough to eat. Foraged wild mushrooms such as chanterelles and morels would be lovely to have—and have them I did at the Rialto market when I lived in Venice—but they rarely appear fresh in my Sarasota, Florida, market. If fresh, frilly chanterelles come your way, their color must be a bright orange, they should be free of slime, and their fragrance, for which they are prized, may suggest peaches or apricots. Don't let dried chanterelles tempt you. Some foraged mushrooms dry beautifully; chanterelles do not. Dried morels, on the other hand, can be quite good, and mostly free of the sand that, when they are fresh, infiltrates the honeycomb of a morel's spongelike pointy cap.

The paragon of foraged mushrooms, with whose texture and fragrance other mushrooms cannot compete, is *Boletus edulis*, familiarly known by its Italian name porcini. It is found growing spontaneously in many parts of the world, where it expresses the character of the territory from which it has sprung. I used to look forward to finding freshly foraged porcini from Borgotaro, in my native Emilia-Romagna, heaped high on a market stall. Borgotaro is also the legally protected name of its mushroom, and you may find it on packets of exquisite dried porcini imported from Italy.

Fresh porcini grow in American woods as well, but there are only a few markets that sell them. You can buy both domestic and imported fresh porcini online, where they are also available frozen. What is even more interesting for a cook, however, is that porcini are widely available dried. The drying of porcini has created a product whose aroma is far more intense than it was when the mushroom was fresh.

Dried porcini must be soaked in water for an hour or more before you cook with them. The more water the better, because after the rehydrated mushrooms are scooped out and the water is strained to filter it clean of grit, you have a fragrant porcini broth with many uses in cooking: in making a mushroom risotto, in any meat braise or stew that needs liquid, or for bestowing porcini aroma on other mushrooms.

The traditional method that Italians use for cooking porcini can be applied to all mushrooms to enrich their flavor. Described in Italian as *trifolati*, the sequence is easily summarized: olive oil, garlic, parsley, the mushrooms, salt, fast heat followed by low, slow heat. Lightly mashed garlic cloves are sautéed in a skillet with olive oil, parsley is added, fresh cleaned mushrooms, cut up or sliced, are dropped into the pan, they are sprinkled with just a little salt to encourage them to shed their liquid, a lid goes over them, the heat is high, and quickly the mushrooms fill the pan with the liquid they produce. When no more liquid is being shed, the lid is removed, the heat is turned down to medium-low, and the mushrooms cook very slowly for perhaps thirty minutes, until they become dark, glossy, and very soft. If you are cooking large portobello caps, you can skip the part about shedding liquid over high heat. Sauté minced garlic in olive oil, then cook the cap at medium-low heat without turning it until it is tender and dark. Sprinkle with parsley, salt, and serve.

Before I cook mushrooms, I always wash them—rehydrated dried porcini included—under fast-running cold water, and then I quickly pat them dry with absorbent paper towels. Both cultivated and foraged mushrooms, when they are fresh and firm and unwashed, keep well for up to a week in the refrigerator, stored loosely in a cloth or brown paper bag. I have found that cremini and white button mushrooms also keep well in the unopened plastic-wrapped container in which they come from the supermarket. Dried porcini keep for a year or more in the refrigerator in a tightly closed tin or jar.

ONIONS

Le Cipolle

Rare is the day in my kitchen that I don't call on an onion to perform. It is the bass player in the combo of flavors that I am putting together, the rhythm section that sets and drives the pace of its fellows. At times it will even come forward to perform a duet as in *fegato alla veneziana*, Venetian liver and onions, and occasionally a captivating solo as in the pasta composed solely of caramelized onions that I developed for one of my earliest cookbooks.

Of the many varieties of onion, the one I always have at hand and use most frequently is the dry, yellow storage onion. Caramelizing onions isn't something I want to do for every dish, but when I do, a yellow onion produces the nuttiest result. For sweating onions—lightly salting them and softening them at medium-low heat under a lid   I also like the delicacy, the aromas of white onions, which are usually larger than the common yellow ones. I hardly ever use red onions, which have a sharp back taste, unless I am using them raw, drawn by the appeal of their color, in a salad such as the classic one with tinned Mediterranean tuna in olive oil and warm cannellini or cranberry beans. I understand that some farmers are beginning to grow the incomparable torpedo-shaped Calabrian red onion, *la cipolla di Tropea*. When that becomes available, it will be an important source of rich flavor, whether cooked, made into jam, or used raw.

I don't buy sweet onions too often. They are more perishable than conventional onions, particularly in a Florida kitchen. When I do get them, and I particularly look forward to the local Florida sweets that look like fat-bellied, giant scallions, I keep them in the refrigerator. Sweet onions are most useful in salads, and I can sweeten any onion for that purpose. Using a very sharp knife, I cut a peeled onion into the thinnest possible slices. I put these in a large strainer and run cold water over them, squeezing them for twenty or thirty seconds, then transfer them to a bowl filled with cold water. I squeeze them again until I see the water becoming milky. I then drain them, refill the bowl with fresh cold water, and put the onion slices back into the bowl. I repeat this operation once or twice over the next half hour or more. It's a method that will take the edge off the bite of any onion, including the red. Before adding the slices to a salad, I pat them as dry as I can between paper towels. I follow the same procedure with diced onion, if that is what I want in a salad.

My favorite onions in Italy, the small, flat cipolline, no broader than a silver dollar, are now being grown in America, where they are called cipollini. (I don't understand the reason for changing the endings of Italian words, *lasagna* instead of *lasagne*, *linguini* instead of *linguine*, *scaloppini* instead of *scaloppine*. What was wrong with using the original correct ending?) Cipolline, or cipollini, are the most delicious little onions for a stew, or as a side dish on their own, or pickled. The only drawback for the cook is that their very thin skin is hard to remove without mangling the onion. Some people blanch the onions first, but that is too much trouble, I find. Using the skinny blade of a small paring knife, I start at the stem end and slip the blade under the first layer of thin, papery skin, pulling it down to the root end. When I have reached the onion's tender core, I complete the preparation, cutting off both the stem and the root ends.

I also like very large Spanish onions, which I choose as flat as I can find. I cut them in half across their middle, but I don't peel them. With the point of a very sharp knife, I cut a crosshatched pattern in the exposed flesh. I sprinkle with salt, add a drop of lemon juice to each side, spreading it with my fingers, pour good olive oil liberally trying to force some of it in between the cuts, and top it off with a fresh grinding of black pepper. The onion goes, cut side facing up, in a baking dish and into a 400° oven, cooking until tender when tested with a fork, about thirty to forty minutes.

When mincing an onion, I may find that I need only part of it. I leave the skin on the unused part, wrap it tightly in plastic wrap (I like the Glad Press'n Seal brand best for this purpose), put the wrapped onion in a resealable plastic bag, and refrigerate it in the vegetable drawer. It will keep for a week or longer.

Take a very close look at the onions you buy. Make sure there are no black or soft spots, particularly at the root end. The skin should cling close to the bulb, which should feel heavy for its size.

English peas

PEAS

I Piselli

Allow me to dispense immediately with the myth that frozen peas are a valid substitute for fresh peas. It depends of course on what you want food to provide. The taste of very young fresh peas—in dishes that illustrate the Italian genius for cooking vegetables such as the Tuscan *pisellini e prosciutto,* tiny peas braised with prosciutto and olive oil, the Roman *vignarola* or Sicilian *frittedda,* similar spring preparations in which peas cook in olive oil together with seasonally young small artichokes and fava beans, or the Venetian soupy risotto, *risi e bisi* the taste of those peas is the most enchanting in the whole vegetable kingdom. And it cannot be produced with frozen peas.

Tiny peas—*pisellini* or *petits pois* in French—are delightful, but size is not quite as important as freshness. It's freshness that delivers the sweetness, because the moment peas are picked their sugar begins to change to starch. Peas need to be absolutely freshly picked and very young, and then they are delicious, bursting crunchily in the mouth with sweet juice, the flavor of one's childhood.

Choose peas by their pods, which must be a dewy green and full. Pop one open. It should snap. Taste the peas; they should be juicy, not floury. If you have the good fortune to acquire really fresh peas, cook them that day if possible. Or keep them two or three days at most in the refrigerator, unshelled and loose in a plastic bag.

Braising fresh peas with romaine lettuce and onions is a dish I learned to make in Rome, where we once lived. Shell the peas, slice an onion very thin, shred several large green leaves of romaine, put everything in a saucepan with olive oil and a pinch of salt, cover, and cook at medium heat. The lettuce should provide all the liquid the peas need, and if they are very fresh they should be done in fifteen or twenty minutes. If they take longer and need a little more liquid, add a spoonful or two of water. Serve immediately or warm up gently before bringing to the table.

Frozen peas? They are quite serviceable in meat braises and stews, with meatballs, in a pasta sauce, or in soups.

PEPPERS

I Peperoni

Sweet bell peppers come to the market in many shades, of which the desirable colors for Mediterranean cooking are red and yellow. A not fully ripened pepper is green. At one time in this country, green was the default color for bell peppers, whereas in Italy's market stalls then, it rarely appeared. Green describes not only the color of the pepper, but its taste. It is not disagreeable; one may even find it pleasantly, if pointedly, vegetal, but it lacks the sweetness that red or yellow peppers have when sautéed or fried and with which they enrich a sauce, a braise, or a soup.

Choose a pepper by its size, shape, and heft. It should be large, heavy, shiny, firm, and cubical in form. The long tapered ones are not as solidly meaty. Examine the skin and pass up any with bruises or cracks or soft spots. A sound, unblemished pepper will keep in good condition for nearly a week if refrigerated in the vegetable drawer. You may store it there loose or in an open plastic bag.

The only thing that a cooked bell pepper's skin contributes to taste is a faint bitterness and the annoying sensation of a papery foreign object in the mouth. If you are making stuffed peppers, you must leave the skin on to hold the hollowed out pepper in shape. Otherwise, a discriminating cook peels peppers before cooking. Cut them lengthwise along the furrows, pry them apart, and remove the seeds and white pith. Shave away the peel with a swiveling blade peeler. You can use the resulting skinless, fleshy strips of pepper as they are or, if the recipe requires it, cut them into squares or dice.

If you are going to eat the pepper raw, remove the skin by charring it over a charcoal flame, or under a broiler, or directly over a gas burner. When the side against the heat blackens, turn the pepper with a pair of tongs. When it is charred on all sides, close it up in a plastic bag. Let it steam awhile inside the bag, and when it is cool enough to hold, take it out and pull off the skin. It will come away easily in shreds. Split open the pepper, remove the white pith and seeds, and cut it lengthwise into broad fillets. Lay these flat on a plate, sprinkle with salt, and cover with olive oil. It is the simplest and most delectable thing you can do with a vegetable. If you prepare the fillets ahead of time, refrigerate them, but be aware that they will taste incomparably better the day you've made them, never having known the refrigerator's chill.

POTATOES

Le Patate

Don't take potatoes for granted. Select your favorite variety as carefully as you would another vegetable: Look at it, hold it, turn it over, press it. The potato you take home should be clean and very hard. No spongy spots, no indentations, no dark splotches. Buy them of a size, so they'll cook evenly. Except for large, heavy russet baking potatoes that sometimes bear small nicks from the harvesting machines, there should be no cuts in the potato's skin.

Keep potatoes in a cool, airy, dark place, storing them in brown paper bags. If bringing them home in plastic, punch holes in the bag. Don't keep them, as I once did, under the sink, where the hot water running above them can make it too warm. Don't wash them until you are ready to cook them. No potato likes bright light. Their skin may turn green, which means a bitter chemical called solanine has developed. Cut away any decidedly green sections before cooking.

When stored correctly, but for a long while, in a cool, dark place, potatoes will sometimes begin to sprout. They do it because they think they've been planted and prepare to grow. Little sprouts are not serious, but cut them off before cooking.

Potatoes come in many shapes, sizes, and colors, but for cooking purposes they all belong, with some individual variations, to one of two groups, either to those with waxy, moist texture or to the dry, starchy kind.

For salads, side dishes, soups, meat braises, or panfrying, your best choice would be one of the moist, waxy, and low- to medium-starch varieties such as yellow, red, white, fingerling, or Peruvian blue or purple potatoes.

Yukon Gold yellow potatoes or Red Bliss are what I use for an Italian potato salad. Aside from the condiments, an Italian potato salad has just one ingredient: the potatoes. We boil them with their skins on, peel them while still very warm—we don't attach any flavor value whatever to a boiled potato peel—and slice them, before they are cold, into disks that we season with sea salt, high quality red wine vinegar, and our fruitiest olive oil. No, no balsamic. No mayonnaise. With good, waxy, creamy potatoes and well-chosen condiments, this is one of the most satisfying side dishes we can bring to the table.

For baking, for deep-frying, and for fluffy mashed potatoes, you need the floury and dry texture that you find in russet potatoes.

The most ethereal confection that you can produce with potatoes is Italy's gnocchi. The only ingredients that go into gnocchi are potatoes and flour. It takes patience to learn to combine the flour and mashed boiled potato into a dough that can be turned by hand into heavenly gnocchi dumplings. Many cooks, probably most cooks, even otherwise good cooks, add egg to the dough to make it firmer and easier to handle. We call that method *alla parigina* (Paris style), and it isn't a compliment. Good gnocchi are meant to be cloud light, not pellet firm. They don't need much chewing, because they dissolve in the mouth.

There are four ways to sauce gnocchi. The simplest is lots of fine butter and a mound of grated Parmigiano Reggiano. An alternative is a sauce made with Gorgonzola Dolce dissolved over low heat with butter and heavy cream. Yet another way is with a light and fresh tomato sauce, such as my tomato sauce with tomato, butter, and onion that so many cooks are now making. My husband's favorite gnocchi are sauced with basil pesto.

Radishes

RADISHES

I Ravanelli

A radish is an enjoyable way to refresh one's appetite in between courses at dinner. For that purpose, after washing the radish, I trim a little bit off the top to expose its flesh and bring it to the table with the rattail on, together with a little saucer heaped with sea salt. It's unnecessary to peel it, although some like to trim it for decorative purposes. Holding it by the tail, one taps the salt with the radish and eats it in little bites.

Buy salad radishes with their tops on so that you can judge freshness from their leaves. A radish can be spongy—*cai* we call it in the dialect of my town—so it may help to squeeze it hard to check its firmness.

Cut off and discard the tops before storing radishes in the vegetable drawer of the refrigerator. Don't wash any until you are ready to eat it. If I am using it in a salad, I cut off the rattail and slice the radish very thin. If the radishes are truly firm, crisp, and possibly elongated, add them to other vegetables served with one of two traditional Italian dips, one cold, the other hot. The cold one is *pinzimonio* in which you mix salt, a drop or two of red wine vinegar, and good, fruity olive oil in individual small dipping bowls. The hot dip is *bagna cauda*, a vigorous blend of olive oil, butter, garlic, and anchovies.

Rapini/Broccoli rabe

RAPINI aka BROCCOLI RABE

Le Cime di Rapa/I Broccoletti di Rapa

In the flavor spectrum of regional Italian food, bitterness flashes brightly. Anticipating the pungency, and relishing it when it shows up, is essential to the appreciation and enjoyment of the taste of many leaf vegetables, from the north of Italy to the south, from radicchio to rapini. Rapini, with their explicit bitterness, star in a broad repertory of dishes from Apulia and Campania in the south, and from Rome in the center.

The iconic sauce of rapini, garlic, olive oil, chili pepper, and anchovies on orecchiette pasta comes from Apulia. In my experience, the satisfactions of rustic Italian cooking are never more profound than in Apulia's combination of sautéed rapini with pureed dried fava beans. In Naples, blanched rapini are *strascinati*—literal translation, "dragged"—stirred vigorously for several minutes in a skillet with olive oil, chili pepper, and anchovies, then served with sausages or on their own. In Rome, rapini sometimes skip a preliminary blanching and slowly braise in a covered saucepan in olive oil, and of course garlic, with an occasional spoonful of water added to prevent sticking. In my town, on the northern Adriatic shore, blanched, chopped rapini are combined with Savoy cabbage and Swiss chard and sautéed in olive oil and garlic. I serve them as a side dish or on *piadina*—a flat bread—with a fresh, soft cheese.

Rapini stalks are exactly as good as the tops, and it is a pity that many recipes instruct you to discard them. They can be tough, however. After slicing away a very small section from their cut ends, use a swiveling blade peeler to peel the rest.

Wash the vegetable in cold water just before cooking. If unwashed, you can refrigerate it for up to four days in a loose plastic bag.

Select rapini whose leaves are firm and bright green. Pass up any whose tops are wilting or slimy. The buds should be closed. If they are bright yellow they have begun to open, an undesirable sign. The stalks also should be firm and green to the very bottom where they have been cut from the plant.

SPINACH

Gli Spinaci

Blanch spinach, sauté it in garlic and olive oil, and you have a dish that summarizes the simplicity, directness, and satisfaction of vegetables cooked the Italian way. Spinach is a familiar part of all styles of Italian cooking: a *torta rustica* with ricotta from Apulia; a soup of spinach and chickpeas from Friuli; spinach gnocchi in Tuscany; the Riviera's savory Easter cake, *torta pasqualina*; in Venice a risotto with the sweet-tasting spinach grown in the island farms of the lagoon; in Bologna, the loftiest example of burghers' cooking, multilayered green dough lasagne.

Spinach leaves are of two basic types, either puckered or smooth, to which one should add an in-between variety with moderate crinkling. If they are fresh, they are all good, although I find the broad, smooth kind milder and sweeter.

If you are buying fresh loose spinach, choose crisp leaves that are a deep, vivid green, none of which should be wilted or blackened by bruises. Unless you cook it the same day, store it unwashed, wrapping each bunch of spinach in a paper towel and stowing it in a resealable bag. It should stay fresh for four to five days. Do not keep spinach after it's cooked, because it develops an unpleasantly tinny taste.

You must wash the spinach you buy loose in several changes of water before you cook it. Use a large basin that you can empty out frequently until you see no traces of grit settling at its bottom. The crinkly spinach will take more to wash clear of grit than the flat.

In recent years I have been buying prewashed spinach sealed in a plastic box. I can refrigerate the unopened box for up to a week if I have to. At first I used to wash it before cooking it, but packaged spinach has already been triple washed and, as I have learned, does not need to be washed at home. In fact, it is better not to, lest it become contaminated by bacteria present in the kitchen.

Stinging nettles

STINGING NETTLES

Le Ortiche

Why cook with them? They taste good. They resemble spinach, but cooked, they have a firmer, more appealing texture, a brighter color, and an untamed, earthy flavor. Nettles won't sting if you wear gloves while handling them when they are raw. A minute of cooking eliminates their sting.

Pasta verde con le ortiche—green pasta with nettles—is very popular in Emilia-Romagna. Briefly blanch and chop the nettles before kneading them into the dough. You can also serve them, after blanching, sautéed with garlic and olive oil. They are terrific with sausages and beans, in a frittata, or in a risotto.

If you are going to use them in a braise, with pasta, or in a risotto, handle them with gloves and blanch them first in boiling water for one minute. You can safely handle them without gloves afterward. If you are going to chop them and use them raw, as in a frittata batter or in the stuffing of tortelloni, use gloves the entire time that you will be in contact with them until after they are cooked.

SUNCHOKES
aka JERUSALEM ARTICHOKES

I Topinambur

This sweet root of sunflowers has long been in search of a name. Italians have called it a Canadian potato or a cane truffle, but oddly, nearly everyone in Italy now refers to it as *topinambur*, the name of an indigenous Brazilian tribe. In America it used to be known as Jerusalem artichoke, but its growers have decided to adopt the name sunchoke, which they have registered. A pity that so fine an ingredient has had to struggle for identity.

The sunchoke, as we now call it, is a knobby, twisty tuber that, to the uninformed, looks like ginger. When I first arrived from Italy, I was one of the uninformed. I had never seen ginger; I thought I had found what I knew as *topinambur*. "I'll have a pound of it, please," I told the greengrocer. What I eventually did with all that ginger I no longer recall.

Choose the tubers first by their color. A clear, unblemished, creamy brown shade is a good indication of freshness. Sunchokes absorb humidity quickly, so feel them for firmness, avoiding those with soft spots and wrinkled skins. If I am going to use them the same week I have bought them, I keep them loose in the refrigerator's vegetable drawer. To keep the tubers another week, or at most two, I wrap them in paper towels and refrigerate them in an open plastic bag.

Sunchokes have a tough skin, but if you are cooking them in a soup, where they form flavorful liaisons with other vegetables such as asparagus or mushrooms, or if you are eating them raw because they are so juicy and nutty, you might not need to peel them, on condition that the tubers are very fresh, and their skin has not turned leathery. Scrub them hard with a rough cloth or brush under cold water and slice them very thin using a sharp chef's knife or a mandoline or the food processor's fine slicing disk. The skin becomes an impediment, however, to full enjoyment of sunchokes' creamy texture and almond-like flavor when you sauté them, braise them, or in what may be the most irresistible display of their merits, bake them with butter under a blanket of grated Parmesan. In these instances, cut off the most troublesome bumps and use the swiveling blade peeler to remove their skin. Blanch them whole and always slice them into very thin disks before proceeding to other cooking methods.

Swiss chard

SWISS CHARD

La Bieta

The many uses of Swiss chard take us to some of the most satisfying moments in the cooking of the Mediterranean, and particularly of Italy. Both the broad, firm, dark green leaves and the meaty stalks of mature chard find much useful employment in an Italian kitchen. The whole chard, blanched and cut up, may end in a *torta rustica* with prosciutto, hard-boiled eggs, grated Parmesan, and herbs. The leaves alone are combined with ricotta for the filling of homemade tortelloni. Leaves and stalks go into a minestrone, or a frittata, or a *sformato* baked with ham and béchamel. The stalks can be prepared as a separate dish, washed, trimmed of strings, and baked with butter and Parmesan cheese. Or fried. When we lived in Rome, we would sometimes have the city's chard panino: Blanched chard leaves are chopped and added to garlic, mashed anchovies, chili pepper, and tomatoes cooked in olive oil and when done are served between two thick slices of grilled bread. In my hometown, we sauté chard chopped together with Savoy cabbage and rapini in garlic and olive oil and spread it over *piadina*, a pizzalike flat bread.

The two common varieties of Swiss chard have either red

or white stalks. The white are preferable because they are meatier and lend themselves better to independent uses. Make sure the leaves are firm, not wilted, and free of bruises. At home, separate the leaves and stalks and refrigerate the stalks in a resealable plastic bag. They will keep for a week. The leaves, however, won't be at their best after two or three days. Refrigerate them separately in a loose plastic bag. Before cooking, wash the leaves in two or three changes of cold water. Unless you are adding them to a liquid medium such as a soup, blanch them very briefly in liberally salted water. The stalks must be blanched separately in boiling water with just a pinch of salt. If they are very broad, as they sometimes are in mature chard, split them in two lengthwise before cooking.

TOMATOES

I Pomodori

Which is it to be, sauce tomatoes or salad tomatoes? Their paths may even converge, but let's think about sauce tomatoes first. Tomato sauce is not all there is to Italian cooking, yet, in its infinite variety, in its animated application to seafood dishes, to the cooking of vegetables, to meat braises, and finally to pasta, the transformation of tomatoes into sauce may be the Italian art of cooking's happiest achievement.

Now the question is which tomato? Poor tomatoes do not make good sauce. Examples abound in pizzerias, restaurants, and home kitchens. When they are ripe and firm-fleshed, I like to use fresh tomatoes, which produce a sauce with fruity exuberance. The plum tomato, of which Roma is the universally available variety, is my first choice. It has few seeds, its cylindrical form is solidly packed with flavorful meaty flesh, and it is a sturdy tomato, which makes it easier to handle and ship, hence it is picked at a riper stage than the other tomatoes in the market. With good plum tomatoes you can make one of the cardinal Italian sauces, the pure Neapolitan *filetto di pomodoro*, tomato fillet. Peel raw, ripe tomatoes with a swiveling blade peeler, cut the tomatoes lengthwise, cut off

*Skin a tomato with
a peeler's swiveling blade.*

the ends, scoop out the seeds, and cut them into long strips, the fillets. Cook these fillets in olive oil, turning them without mashing them too much, letting them become sauce while maintaining some of their original fleshy consistency.

Another fresh variety suitable for sauce is the small, round, globe tomato usually sold in clusters attached to a length of its vine. It may be labeled "vine-ripened," a misleading description because it acquires its intense ripe-red color after it has been picked. To make a good sauce, it must be cooked longer than a ripe Roma. A similar, smaller variety called Campari, which is sweet and juicy, also makes good sauce, but the peeling of it takes patience. To peel these and other fresh tomatoes for any sauce except the Neapolitan *filetto* described above, I plunge them in boiling water for less than a minute. A longer hot bath is not necessary and would undermine their consistency, making them too watery.

To make a sauce with great depth of flavor, the genuine canned, peeled Italian San Marzano tomatoes are matchless. *Genuine* is a necessary word, because there are many imitations, packed both in this country and in Italy, all of them inferior. Authentic San Marzanos are grown only in the valley of the Sarno River near Salerno. They are described on the label as *Pomodoro S. Marzano dell'Agro Sarnese-Nocerino* and bear the designation DOP, which certifies their legally protected origin.

The San Marzano, like the Roma, is a plum tomato, tapered at the stem end, with a slimmer, longer body than the Roma. It has few seeds, and the taste of its dense flesh is the fruitiest, most intense of any plum tomato. The cans come in two sizes, and if you are not always cooking for a crowd, it would be convenient to stock both sizes and use the smaller one when you don't need to make too much sauce. If you have San Marzanos left over in the can, transfer them to a glass jar, float a very small amount of olive oil on top, screw a cap on tightly, and refrigerate. They should keep well for a week or more.

In other areas near Naples they cultivate and pack small, round, unpeeled tomatoes, *pomodorini*. These are excellent for a lighter sauce, but they must be strained to remove their tough skins.

Beefsteak is the classic salad tomato, a true fruit of summer, juicy and richly tomatoey in its season, mealy and flavorless out of it. I like using it alone in garlic-scented seasoning. Peel and mash a clove or two of garlic, sprinkle it lightly with sea salt, and let it soak in red wine vinegar for at least thirty minutes. Peel and cut the tomato, sprinkle very little salt on it, and pour the scented vinegar over it, holding back the garlic. Drizzle olive oil over the tomato, turning it two or three times.

An excellent variety of beefsteak that I have sometimes come across is the Brandywine, exceptionally full-flavored. The list of beefsteak varieties is endless. Because of its climate, Florida produces a type of beefsteak under the registered name Ugly Ripe that is available most of the year. It is the tastiest tomato in our supermarket, but its deeply ridged shape is uneven, which apparently makes it look ugly to some. Costoluto is a tomato variety of Italian origin, also uneven in shape and heavily ridged. In Italy costoluto is known as a Florentine tomato; in America it has become Genoese. It is delicious and very good for making sauce as well as using in a salad.

The prevalent tomato shape in the stores and in the markets is the smooth-skinned, evenly round globe. It rarely has much flavor. I'd rather use Romas than globes for a salad.

The miniature tomatoes in cherry, grape, or pear shapes have had sweetness bred into them and are consequently very agreeable in a salad. I slice them in half so that they can better pick up salt.

Tomatoes of many colors—pink, yellow, green, brown—are sold as heirlooms, although the beefsteaks are also heirlooms. Sometimes they are very, very good, but their shelf life is short, and if they don't sell quickly, they become too soft for my taste. In a salad tomato I look not only for ripeness, but also for firmness. Mushy I don't like.

All tomatoes going into a salad, except for the miniatures, should be peeled raw, using a swiveling blade vegetable peeler. The skin is bitter, its texture holds no pleasure, and if taste is a criterion, it should be eliminated. I also believe that a tomato cut into irregular wedges soaks up seasoning better than when it is cut into thin, even, round slices.

The tomatoes you buy should have no cracks, no soft spots, no dark splotches. They should have a decidedly earthy, almost farmyard scent, which you can pick up from the end

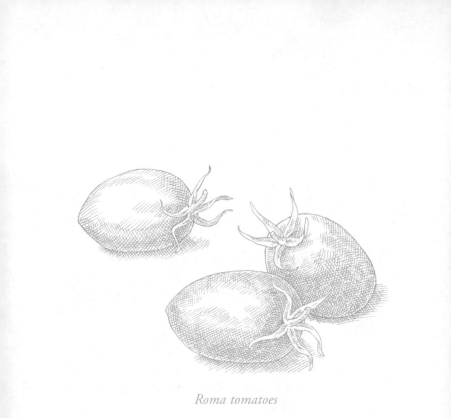

Roma tomatoes

opposite the stem. Be watchful at checkout when they are bagging your carefully chosen tomatoes. Don't let them pack them together with any hard, heavy, or sharp-edged objects. It is best to ask that the tomatoes go separately into a bag of their own. Do not store tomatoes in the refrigerator. Store them at room temperature in a dark corner, their stem ends up. Feel them gently from time to time to make sure they are not becoming too soft. If they are cut or cracked, refrigerate them for at most a couple of days in a resealable plastic bag. If you are putting them in a salad, bring them to room temperature first.

Shave white truffles with a steel truffle slicer.

TRUFFLES

I Tartufi

A truffle is a fungus, but that doesn't make it a mushroom, because even though a mushroom is also a fungus, not every fungus is a mushroom. Mushrooms rise out of the ground; truffles lurk beneath it, out of sight but within range of a dog's trained nose. Dogs are a better choice than pigs, which some countries use, because a dog denies itself the pleasure of eating the truffle it has just dug up, whereas—if not opportunely restrained—the pig will gobble it up.

The white and the black truffle are the two most desirable and most valuable truffles; the winter *bianchetto* and the summer *scorzone* truffles are two lesser, but useful varieties, whereas at a much lower level there are several other kinds whose contributions, in terms of flavor and aroma, are negligible.

The white truffle of Alba grows wild in the Piedmontese woods, and it may also be unearthed in other regions of northern and central Italy. Attempts to cultivate it have failed, allowing it to become, by a considerable spread, the most expensive single food harvested from the ground. It is worth the price to one who is swayed by the penetrating, musky aroma that shavings of freshly harvested white truffle bestow on pasta or risotto. If you fancy white truffles, you must get a steel truffle slicer, which will quickly and evenly blanket a plate of tagliatelle or risotto with shavings from the precious nugget.

White truffles dispense their aroma most effusively when raw, but if they are very fresh, they can have a notable impact on cooking. In one of the rare Italian dishes with turkey, Bologna celebrates the truffle season with a cutlet of turkey breast sautéed in butter and layered with prosciutto and white truffle. I celebrate my husband's birthday, which happily for him comes during the heart of the truffle season, with a baked *tortino al tartufo.* It is composed of a layer of peeled, sliced, boiled potatoes covered by truffle shavings, topped with slivers of Parmigiano-Reggiano, and dotted in turn with butter. Several such layers mount up in sequence toward a crown of grated Parmigiano-Reggiano and butter.

The white truffle season begins in mid-September and ends after Christmas. The latter half of its season coincides with the start of the black truffle season, which runs from mid-November to March. The black truffle is less expensive than the white, but it is nonetheless the most precious crop when it is at the peak of its season. It grows in central Italy, in Périgord in the southwest of France, in Spain, and in many other countries. Its aroma is not pungent; it is gently earthy, woodsy, and quite satisfying. I shave black truffles into slivers or grate them, depending on what I want to make. A pasta dish called *alla nursina*—"in the style of Norcia," a town in the center of black truffle production in Umbria—is the best foil for the truffle's earthiness and depth. The sauce is brilliantly simple: You mince garlic very fine, brown it lightly in olive oil, put in some chili pepper, dissolve two or three mashed anchovy fillets in the oil, and off heat, just as you are about to drop the drained hot pasta into the pan, swirl the gratings of a good-size truffle into the sauce. Grating is tedious; I prefer to throw the whole truffle into the food processor, which pulverizes it in seconds.

Unlike white truffles, which resist cultivation, it has been relatively simple to grow black truffles. It only takes time—time to raise, in suitable soil and a favorable climate, a grove of oak trees to whose roots the truffle's spores attach themselves. The Australian island of Tasmania has entered black truffle production with great promise. Its cold months are June to August, so Tasmania now brings us the wintry pleasures of black truffles to delight our summers.

From mid-January to the beginning of April, a new white truffle crop comes to the market. These are called *bianchetti* truffles, a more modest variety than the autumnal Alba truffles. Their aroma is feebler, yet distinctly garlicky and spicy. If you buy a jar of truffled condiment that is described as made with white truffles, it is probably produced with *bianchetti.*

From the beginning of May to the end of August, while waiting for the Alba truffle season to begin, one can satisfy one's longings with a dark summer variety called *scorzone.* It is a knobby, black nugget with a marbled, medium brown interior. Its subdued aroma is less reminiscent of any other truffle than it is of mushrooms.

A truffle's aroma is its sole desirable feature, and the intensity of that aroma is the clue to the truffle's freshness, a clue that must guide your purchase. Don't buy truffles too long before you intend to use them. The black will keep better than the white, but none will keep for longer than a few days, and none can maintain their scent unaltered for even that long. Do not store truffles in rice unless you are interested only in infusing rice with truffle aromas. If you cannot use a truffle the day you buy it, wrap it in butcher paper or a paper towel and store it in a large glass jar on the lowest level of the refrigerator. A truffle needs to be kept dry. If you are going to keep it another day or two, unwrap it, discarding the paper, rub the truffle with a clean toothbrush, and rewrap it with clean, dry paper.

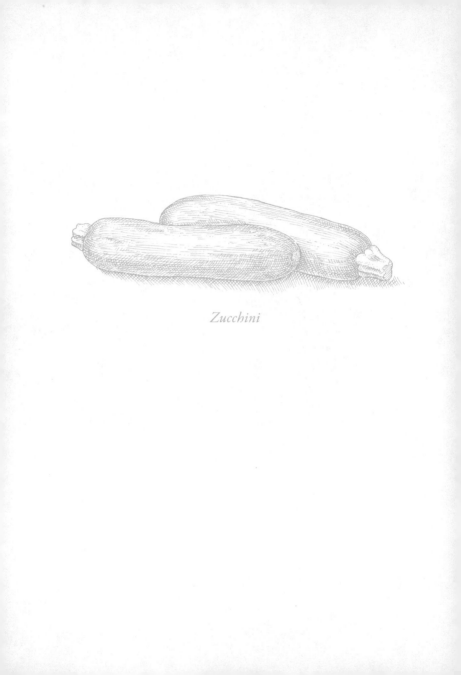

Zucchini

ZUCCHINI

Le Zucchine

With few and uncommon variations, zucchini come in two shades of green, one dark, the other pale. I prefer the paler version when I can get it, because it has a richer, fuller taste. Size is important. Very large zucchini are watery and bland, while the appeal of a baby vegetable is prevalently ornamental. Choose zucchini that are about one and a half inches thick and not more than seven inches long. The skin should be glossy and free of nicks, scrapes, and dents. Look at the end that was attached to the stem. If part of the stem is still attached, its color should be fresh, not darkened by age. Fresh zucchini are firm, unyielding to pressure.

If truly fresh, they will keep in the vegetable drawer of the refrigerator for a week. Keeping them loose rather than in a bag will better maintain their crispness. Zucchini skin is very soft, and grit can easily become embedded in it, particularly in zucchini purchased directly from farmers. To prepare them for cooking, I always soak uncut zucchini in cold water for at least fifteen minutes, then scrub them under running water with a rough cloth or a vegetable brush.

I can't think of a vegetable with greater versatility than

zucchini. It can be fried, sautéed, grilled, boiled, or baked; it can be cooked whole, sliced, shredded, or hollowed out and stuffed. There are two types of the tool you need for hollowing out zucchini. One is fully cylindrical with a cutting edge at its tip; the other is half of a cylinder ending in a sharp point. The latter is more maneuverable and does a better job. When you hollow out zucchini, keep the core you have removed to use in a frittata with caramelized onions and grated Parmesan. Of the many stuffings that zucchini may contain, one of my favorites is composed of ground meat, preferably lamb, but also pork and beef mixed, and rice. Once stuffed, I brown them in butter or olive oil, depending on the inclination of the moment, with onion sliced very fine, then I braise them slowly with tomatoes.

The blossoms of the zucchini or squash plant are also edible. The bright yellow flower that emerges directly from the ends of the zucchini as they issue from the plant is the female blossom. A second, slightly smaller flower is attached to a slender stalk that grows from the stem of the plant. It is the male blossom. The blossoms you choose for the kitchen must be firm, not limp, and both the petals and the pistils must be colored a very bright yellow. Remove the pistils, because they are slightly bitter. The stalk of the male flower is not edible, but one may want to keep it as a convenient handle.

There are recipes in which zucchini or squash blossoms are folded around a variety of ingredients and sautéed or baked. A terrible waste, I think. Nothing capitalizes so perfectly on the texture of the flower, transforming it into a crisp yet diaphanous biteful, as dipping it in a plain batter of flour and water or flour and beer and quickly deep-frying it in lard or in a neutral-tasting vegetable oil.

THE ESSENTIAL
PANTRY

La Dispensa Essenziale

Spaghettoni, spaghetti, spaghettini

PASTA

La Pasta Compera

On a book tour, the food editor of the local newspaper remarked, hoping to demonstrate her devotion to the best in Italian cuisine, "I only ever use fresh pasta."

"You don't know what you are missing," I replied.

The one useful notion that someone cooking pasta the Italian way ought to hold on to has also been the most difficult to grasp for most of the people I speak to, food writers included. Fresh pasta, so inappropriately described, for it can be dry and months old, is not superior to boxed pasta. It is merely different.

There are two broad groups of pasta; one is made from flour and eggs, the other from flour and water. The first, in its finest version, is made at home from hand-kneaded dough opened up into a flat sheet with a long, narrow, hardwood pasta roller. The sheets are cut either into noodles of various widths or into small square, round, triangular, or half-moon sections that one will fold and close around a nugget of meat, cheese, and/or vegetable stuffing to make filled pasta dumplings. There are also shapes of homemade pasta, such as orecchiette, trofie, cavatelli, and busiate, produced entirely by hand, pinching, poking, turning, or squeezing dough.

The other pasta group is an industrial product. A dough of hard wheat flour—semolina—and water is kneaded mechanically and forced through dies that will squeeze it into one of scores of different shapes, from spaghetti to rigatoni to strozzapreti to small soup pasta. After it is dried hard, it is boxed and shipped to stores.

Pasta rolled out at home from egg dough and factory-made extruded pasta absorb different sauces. Please stop to think about that. It is extremely important, because it opens up access to the vast range of Italian pasta dishes. There are sauces that are far more enjoyable on factory-made rather than homemade pasta and that work better with one shape rather than another. When matched to its most appropriate sauces, the flavors of store-bought, factory-made boxed pasta are fully as remarkable and satisfying as those of the homemade variety.

Take spaghetti, for example. A perfect match for it is the simple tomato sauce that I make with butter and an onion. It is my family's comfort dish. Spaghetti goes so well with vegetable sauces such as eggplant and ricotta, fried zucchini with garlic and basil, caramelized onions, sauces that it can curl around or those that it can cling to, such as carbonara. Meat sauce, however, sits awkwardly on those long, narrow strands, notwithstanding the British elevation of spaghetti Bolognese—spag bol—to national dish status.

Spaghettini—thin spaghetti—is a shape that, for reasons impenetrable to me, is impossible to find except online and occasionally in a few stores that focus on Italian specialties.

It's a great pity, because it is the perfect vehicle for clam sauce and other seafood sauces and for any sauce based on olive oil. Olive oil sauces, which provide the perfect coating for the smooth surfaces of spaghettini, are an awkward choice for the absorbent, porous texture of homemade egg pasta, which longs instead for butter and cream.

Another factory-made shape, bucatini, the hollow spaghetti, has forever been wedded to amatriciana sauce. Penne, shells, fusilli, all short tube or concave shapes, are drawn to sauces whose morsels they can pull inside them, sauces such as those with sausages, with mushrooms, with cut-up asparagus, with bell peppers. Large tubes like rigatoni have the ideal shape for holding meat sauce and for enduring baking in an oven.

Not all boxed factory pasta is of equally wonderful quality. The shelves of every supermarket I have ever walked into are piled high with mediocre brands. How much difference can there be between one box of penne and another? A lot! There are many decisions that the artisan must make in the process of transforming milled grain into pasta in a box, and each decision represents a variable in quality, in taste, in texture, in cooking time, in the capacity to absorb sauce. The first decision is about where to source the wheat, which must, by tradition and by law, be hard wheat, also known as semolina or durum wheat. That first decision has a huge influence on the consistency and individual character of a pasta brand. Some producers exert control by growing their own wheat, others, through the contracts they stipulate with growers in Italy or abroad. Martelli's pasta, than which there is none better, is made from the North American grain they have used for decades.

The remaining steps in the aim for quality essentially consist of slowing things down: in slow, lengthy kneading; in slow extrusion of the dough through bronze dies that impart a rough, sauce-thirsty texture on the surface of the spaghetti, penne, rigatoni, fusilli, every shape coming through; in the unhurried tempo of the drying rooms, where low temperatures keep pasta drying for several days.

The great pasta artisans have their plants in central and southern Italy. Martelli is in Tuscany; Cocco in Abruzzo; Cavalieri in the southernmost tip of Apulia; Faella near Naples, in Gragnano, the birthplace of Italian pasta; and Molini del Ponte in Sicily, where Filippo Drago mills ancient Sicilian hard grains. These are some of the most prominent, but there are many others.

There are a few more steps to the realization of a perfect dish of pasta, and they take place in your kitchen. If you are feeding four, you need a pot that will hold four to five quarts of water. When the water boils, it must be salted. I use two tablespoons of table salt or Diamond Crystal kosher salt. A broad pot is better than a narrow one, because, when the water boils, you can drop in a pound of spaghetti that will immediately lie flat and be fully submerged without your having to bend the strands below the water's level.

Pasta should be cooked at a sustained boil until it is tender, yet firm to the bite. It used to be that people cooked their pasta too long. Now they are likely to cook it not long enough. Ignore absurdly low cooking times printed on the package. Cocco, for example, advises nine minutes' cooking for a cut of pasta that takes me fifteen minutes. Pasta is not enjoyable when crunchy. Don't go by the timer. Taste periodically until you are satisfied.

Drain cooked pasta immediately and transfer it to a warm bowl. If you have used butter in the sauce, add grated Parmesan cheese to the pasta, toss quickly, then toss with some fresh butter. Add the sauce and toss, turning the pasta over and over, not once, not twice, but at least a dozen times, thoroughly coating every strand of spaghetti, every penne tube with sauce. Do not serve the dish with a pool of sauce resting on top, however decorative that may appear to be.

If your sauce was made with olive oil, and possibly tomatoes with mashed anchovies, or capers, or olives, you may want to use pecorino romano. If you decide to do so, add the grated romano cheese to the pasta as soon as you have drained and placed it steaming hot in the serving bowl. Toss quickly, then add a spoonful of olive oil and proceed to toss thoroughly.

Chefs like to toss drained pasta for a minute or so over the burner in the skillet containing the sauce, and afterward slide it into the serving bowl. This doesn't work well with all types of pasta. Yes with spaghetti, no with hollow tubes. The consistency of such shapes as penne, ziti, or rigatoni deteriorates in a hot skillet; it becomes gummy, a little like the precooked pasta that is reheated and served in bad Italian restaurants. It lacks the fresh, spontaneous taste of home cooking; there is a slick, professional patina to it that I don't like. On the other hand, a homemade egg noodle, like fettuccine, should be tossed in a pan with a sauce of gorgonzola, butter, and heavy cream, which it loves to drink up.

I actually prefer a platter to a deep bowl for tossing and serving pasta, in particular the tender, homemade kind. When spread on a long platter, you get more even distribution of sauce, and the pasta does not risk becoming soggy as it may at the bottom of a deep bowl.

There are cooks who use an appliance at home to extrude pasta in imitation of the industrial process. It extrudes egg and flour dough through dies to form shapes typical of boxed store pasta, such as penne. The product has neither the finesse of home-rolled pasta nor the textural substance of factory pasta. It is a hybrid, and not a successful one.

If you love fettuccine, tagliatelle, or pappardelle but don't want to, or can't, make them yourself, there are dried, boxed, commercial versions that rival, and perhaps surpass, the egg pasta that many cooks are capable of making at home. A small hilly town of two thousand souls in the Marche, a pastoral region facing the Adriatic Sea in central Italy, has become the source of commercially produced egg pasta of very high quality. The town is Campofilone, and the most notable producer of its pasta is Ivana Maroni.

RISOTTO RICE

Il Riso da Risotto

Every language has a word for rice. In Italian it's *riso*. But there is no other word, in any language, for risotto, the rich, creamy transformation of rice into a dish almost limitless in its variety that northern Italian cooks began to produce about two hundred years ago.

The unique consistency of risotto has its source in slow, continual stirring of rice over moderate heat to release some of its starch. Only a handful of Italian rice varieties suit the risotto method, and one can limit one's acquaintance to the three most important ones: Arborio, Carnaroli, and Vialone Nano. These are their varietal names, for each of which there are several producers.

Arborio rice has long established its popularity with cooks both in Italy and abroad. Its plump, large grains are packed with starch, of which a substantial amount will dissolve to produce risotto with luscious texture. It demands watchfulness in the dosage of liquid and careful timing. Overcooked Arborio makes gummy risotto.

Carnaroli, which was created in 1945 from a cross between Vialone and a Japanese strain, is the finest variety for risotto. Its handsome, large kernel is sheathed in soft starch that dissolves deliciously as you stir, while the core of tough starch expands visibly as it absorbs broth, cooking to a firm, satisfying, elegant consistency. When I first wrote about it in 1986, Carnaroli was a rare item that few of my readers could then find, but it has since won over so many cooks that its production has drawn close to Arborio's.

There are many excellent producers of Carnaroli, such as Campanini and Beretta, but the outstanding one is Acquerello. Upon harvesting the rice, Acquerello stores the unhusked kernels in a granary at low temperature for a minimum of one year and a maximum of seven before processing it. Aging stabilizes the components of the rice, which hold up better when cooked and more fully absorb the risotto's flavors.

Vialone Nano is the signature variety of risotto in Venice and other cities of the Veneto region. Its kernel is round and stubby and well-endowed with starch. It cooks to an admirable firm consistency and is well-suited to seafood risottos in the Veneto style known as *all'onda* (wavy). There is a version of Vialone Nano, produced with vintage equipment, that bestows a different and enjoyable texture on risotto. In this antique procedure, an oval basin of red Verona marble contains the rice, and old gears made of wood lift and lower wooden poles two yards long to pound the grains, softly husking them. The poles are called *pestelli*, and the rice is known as *riso ai pestelli*. A grainy substance from the gentle husking clings to the rice and eventually slips into the risotto, adding to its texture. One of the producers that still makes Vialone Nano with pestelli is Gazzani, who ships its rice to the online specialist in Italian foods, Gustiamo.

The foundation of nearly every risotto is chopped onion sautéed in butter. At first, the rice is stirred into, and coated by, the hot butter and onion, then it is moistened by a cupful of wine, usually white. After the wine has been absorbed, periodic doses of broth are administered, three or four ladlefuls at a time. The rice is stirred continually while it absorbs the liquid that is added at intervals. Risotto should be cooked in a pan whose heavy bottom is broad enough to spread the rice evenly while stirring it. I use a long-handled wooden spatula whose mixing end is straight with rounded corners. The straight end wipes the bottom of the pan clean as it sweeps it when stirring, and the corners dislodge the rice that likes to gather between the bottom and the sides of the pot. I stir with a circular motion from the center toward the sides.

Marcella's spatula
for stirring risotto

Risotto is not complete without the final *mantecatura* in which, off heat, butter is first whisked into the risotto, and then grated Parmesan cheese. Some cooks omit this step when making a seafood risotto; others make no exception.

Unlike pasta, risotto does not require a warm serving platter, nor should it be eaten flaming hot. It is best served onto an individual flat plate, rather than a bowl. It is a gracious gesture, when serving, for the host or hostess to shake the plate with a circular motion to spread out the risotto so that the guest can eat starting at the edges, where the risotto will be cooler, then proceeding toward the center, where its heat takes longer to abate.

EXTRA VIRGIN OLIVE OIL

L'Olio Extra Vergine d'Oliva

If I were spending time in a habitable but remote outpost, to which I'd have to bring a supply of food that did not exceed five items, these would be dried pasta, canned tuna, canned tomatoes, salted anchovies, and extra virgin olive oil. The single most significant contribution to my survival might well come from the olive oil.

If olive oil were a drug, it would have a place of honor among miracle drugs. No other food in the pantry of our Western kitchen plays a more active part in our well-being at the same time that it brings deep pleasure to our table.

Olive oil is not the only fat I cook with. I come from cow and pig country in the north of Italy, and when I think it's appropriate to the taste and texture of what I am cooking, I cook with butter, and I cook with lard. Read more about both ingredients on pages 179 and 182. Nonetheless, it was my good fortune to have been born and raised in the culinary culture of the Mediterranean, whose flavors like to travel in one commodious vehicle: olive oil.

When I say *olive oil*, I mean extra virgin olive oil—and only extra virgin olive oil. No other grade has its transformative power, its combination of therapeutic antioxidants

Extra virgin olive oil

and flavonoids that is kind to your life, as well as loving to your palate. Italy, along with nearly every other country that produces olive oil, defines extra virgin olive oil as a virgin oil, extracted from olives solely by mechanical means that do not in any way alter the oil, which, when tested, may not contain more than 0.8 percent free oleic acidity. Notwithstanding this apparently unambiguous definition, large industrial processors and packers have somehow, through blending and other manipulations, succeeded in flooding the market with olive oil whose shortcomings should have disqualified it as extra virgin.

A home cook has several strategies available in the pursuit of true extra virgin olive oil. The first step is to respect it, when genuine, as the one product in your pantry on which you can depend for cooking that is both healthful and flavorful. The second step is to buy no olive oil from a supermarket chain. If an olive oil's brand has become familiar to you through advertising, stay away from it. The simplest labels, avoiding picturesque details in favor of straightforward information, are the most credible ones. A fresh olive oil, carefully extracted from locally harvested olives in prime condition, bearing the name of its producer, along with the date of the harvest, and possibly the name of the olive variety and its place of origin, cannot be cheap. A bargain price is no bargain. The best place to buy olive oil is a food specialty store where you can talk to someone who has chosen and can describe the oils for sale. There are also reliable online sources, which I have listed at the back of this book.

Develop an appreciation for the taste of olive oil. Olives are fruits whose oils differ in flavor, varying in intensity from delicate to medium to strong. Some will appeal to you more than others. It could be worth your while to discover which, by organizing a simple tasting for yourself and one or two friends.

You may come across detailed descriptions of the professional method of tasting olive oil, but unless you plan to go into the business, I would ignore them. What matters to a cook is not how olive oil performs out of a blue tasting glass, but how it tastes with food. In one of my cookbooks, I proposed a tasting of no more than four or five different oils, each drizzled on separate slices of plain, peeled, slightly warm, boiled potatoes. I was comforted to find that Italy's *Gambero Rosso* guide to olive oils now recommends the same approach. Collect a few bottles of oils of respectable quality and also a supermarket's least expensive extra virgin, which will serve as a foil. Conceal the identity of all the bottles, enclosing them in numbered paper bags. Have separate plates for the sliced potatoes keyed to the numbers on the bags. Refresh your palate between each taste with sips of water.

The basic attributes by which olive oil is described are fruitiness, pungency, and bitterness. The intensity of each varies according to the variety of olive it was made from and the place where the olives were harvested. An oil extracted from Taggiasca olives on the Riviera will show delicate fruitiness and reduced pungency and bitterness, which has often made it a good choice for fish. An Umbrian oil from the Moraiolo olive is rich in antioxidants and consequently expressive of pungency and bitterness. It is splendid brushed on grilled meats. In Tuscany, the Frantoio olive may lead to intensely flavored oils with bold pungency that are excellent with braised vegetables and soups. I am fond of the south's extra virgin oils, often very fruity, such as the oils from Campania based on the Ortice varietal, or from the Ogliarola olive in Apulia, which is pleasingly aromatic, gently balanced between pungency and bitterness. Sicilian extra virgins range from the intense, sometimes overpowering fruitiness of the oils from the western side of the island derived from the Nocellara del Belice varietal to the Tonda Iblea olive harvested in the hills above Syracuse. Yet Sicily also produces delicately pleasing oil from the Biancolilla olive in the Agrigento zone.

Oils that have been subjected to corrective measures in industrial processing or that have been poorly stored or extracted from partly fermented olives may have various tastes inconsistent with fresh extra virgin oil; they may taste rancid or fusty. The latter is a sensation that to me recalls that of boiled-over milk. The supermarket oil you dropped into the tasting will be helpful in displaying defects.

Do not place too much importance on color, which may range from a golden yellow-green to a deep forest green. Do pay attention to harvest dates. Oil does not age well. You should allow it not much more than two years. Ideally, especially if you are using the oil as a raw condiment, the first four months of an olive oil's life are its most desirable. Extra virgin olive oil suffers from exposure to light. Do not buy it if it comes in a clear bottle. It also suffers from long confinement in a tin can.

Use extra virgin olive oil as liberally as you can afford in your cooking. Do not be distracted by the voices that talk about smoke points. For the record, the smoke point of good-quality extra virgin olive oil is suitable for all but the highest frying temperatures. In any event, I do not deep-fry with olive oil. When I want the food I am frying to make a fresh, light impression on the palate, I do not need the distracting flavor of olive oil. Non-hydrogenated lard would be a better choice. Do not listen to the food scientists who tell you it is pointless to cook with extra virgin olive oil because it loses its precious aromatic qualities. It doesn't lose its aromas; it transfers them to the ingredients that are cooking with it. I adore the richness of extra virgin olive oil when braising vegetables, which, aside from its use on salads, may be its highest calling. In many pasta sauces, particularly those with seafood, such as clams or mussels, using extra virgin olive oil is not subject to question; it is mandatory.

If you make constant use of it, as I do, you may keep a small quantity of extra virgin olive oil within quick reach. Lacking a cold pantry—there are no cold pantries in a Florida condominium—I keep my finest oil, which I use raw as a condiment, in a dark cupboard at a distance from the stove and oven.

PARMIGIANO-REGGIANO

The natural flavor of ingredients—my thoughts go to the ones I have known best in my life: to the vegetables grown in the salt-laden air of the Venetian lagoon's farm islands; to that same lagoon's small shellfish, the razor clams, the tiny soft-shelled crabs, the brown shrimp; to the olive oil from Lake Garda; to the peaches of my native Romagna; to the sweet San Daniele prosciutto from Friuli; to the tender lambs of the Roman Campagna; to the majestic red wines of the Langhe in Piedmont—each brings us the flavor of a single inimitable place. The paramount example of such flavor is that of Parmigiano-Reggiano cheese.

It's about the milk, a milk rich like no other, milk produced by the cows of a small, precisely mapped and legally protected area in northern Italy, enclosed almost entirely by the provinces of Parma and Reggio Emilia, where the country's plushest pasture lies. It's the milk, and the manual method by which it becomes cheese, a method that in nearly eight hundred years has changed only in the hands working it. It's the milk, the method, and the aging, a slow two years' maturation at natural, seasonal temperatures.

It's the taste. Pry off and slowly munch a nugget of Parmigiano. In the warmth of your mouth its grainy texture slowly dissolves. It doesn't feel like a hard cheese; it is an

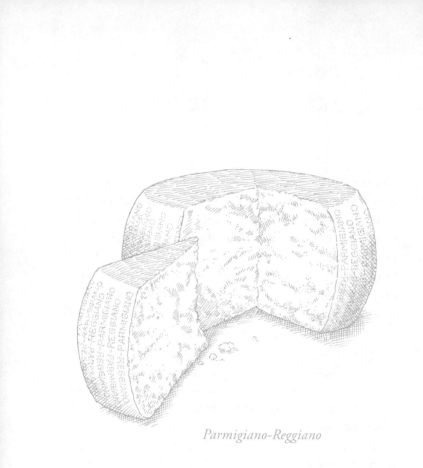

Parmigiano-Reggiano

increasingly creamy complex of satisfying sensations, its fragrant layers of flavor steadily mounting and then tapering to a long, bracing, faintly bitter back taste like that of apricot or peach stones. If up to now you have used Parmigiano-Reggiano only for grating, you will regret having denied yourself the pleasure of one of the greatest of table cheeses.

The thousands of dairies supplying milk to the hundreds of cheese makers that produce Parmigiano-Reggiano labor under the rigorous supervision of the biologists and agronomists of the Consortium, an efficient and authoritarian entity that has emphasized consistency, sometimes at the expense of individual artisanal variations. There are variations nonetheless, largely derived from the season in which the cheese is produced.

The date of production is burned into the rind of the cheese, and you can easily learn it if your cheese monger displays a whole wheel of cheese. The two most significant differences in the seasonal characteristics of Parmigiano-Reggiano are between the summer cheese and the winter cheese. The summer is dryer, grainier, and more pungent. Its consistency and accented flavor are ideal for grating. The winter cheese is milder, richer in butterfat, delicious at table. Some people prefer what they discern as the more balanced flavors of autumn's Parmigiano, others the herbaceous fragrances of the spring cheese. In reality, Parmigiano produced at any time of the year is a superior hard cheese both for table use and for grating.

One enduring, and possibly expanding, variation in Parmigiano character is the cheese derived from the Razza Reggiana breed, otherwise known as the Red Cow. Originally all Parmigiano-Reggiano was made from Red Cow milk, but the dominant breed today is the spotted Friesian breed, a more abundant milk producer. A small resurgence of Red Cow breeding is going on, and its Parmigiano is available at online and retail cheese mongers both. The color of the cheese is yellower, and its flavor is nuttier, grassier, richer, and more emphatic. It is believed to be suitable for aging well beyond the customary twenty-four months. Should you find a source of Parmigiano-Reggiano made from the milk of Red Cows that were grown on mountain pasturage rather than in the plains, you may be onto the ultimate version of a cheese that is the ultimate to begin with.

If you have access to a good cheese monger, buy a wedge of Parmigiano pried fresh from the wheel rather than the plastic-wrapped chunks from the supermarket. The rind you get with it is a bonus, because you can enrich a soup or a braise with a piece or two of it. Examine the opened wheel on display. The cheese should look dewy. If the part against the rind looks chalky, the cheese has been stored badly and is drying out.

When you have found a reliable source of Parmigiano-Reggiano, consider buying a substantial piece of it. If scrupulously stored and refrigerated, it keeps quite well. I can store it for many months before using it up. If the piece you've bought is very large, split it in two or more parts. Wrap it tightly in a layer of good cheesecloth. I buy mine from the King Arthur Baker's Catalogue. Over the cheese-cloth, wrap a sheet of special cheese paper, available from Formaticum, or aluminum foil, fastening it tightly with paper tape. Refrigerate it, enclosing it, if you wish, in a large resealable plastic bag. Rewrap the cheese with a fresh piece of cheesecloth every ten days. If white spots show on the surface, they signal the presence of the amino acids that contribute to the desirable graininess of the cheese. If a few green moldy spots appear, simply scrape them off. If the cheese is beginning to look chalky, it is drying. Replace the cheesecloth with a freshly moistened piece, wrap the cheese in it, wrap aluminum foil over it, and refrigerate overnight to replenish the cheese's moisture. The following day, rewrap it, replacing the moist cheesecloth with a dry piece.

Do not buy grated cheese, nor have a store grate cheese for you, nor grate it at home too long in advance of using it. Once grated, it begins to lose moisture. A way of knowing how an Italian restaurant uses Parmigiano is to ask if you could have a chunk of the cheese to eat at table. It is possible that they do not have any.

Let me introduce you to the crostino of Parmigiano and olive oil that my husband's grandmother used to prepare for him when he was a schoolboy in Bologna. Grill slices of good, plain, crusty bread to a pale brown and lay them on a tray. Blanket the bread with abundant freshly grated Parmigiano, allowing an excess of cheese to drop onto the tray. Pour enough olive oil over it to soak the cheese thoroughly, not caring if some of the oil spills onto the tray. After eating the crostino, use a slice or two of bread to wipe up the oil and cheese from the tray. Your fingers will get sticky. Victor used to lick his.

Grana Padano

Grana is the generic colloquial Italian name for all hard grating cheese with a granular texture. Parmigiano is a type of grana. *Padano* is another. Like Parmigiano, Grana Padano is made from cow's milk, but unlike the milk for Parmigiano, Grana Padano's is produced over a vast zone, spilling over twenty-seven provinces in five northern regions. Its variable territorial origin makes it considerably more inconsistent than Parmigiano, a variability accentuated by the two size formats that are permitted. Parmigiano is allowed only one size wheel. Grana Padano is aged twelve months, half that of Parmigiano. There can be no questioning the superior richness and complexity of Parmigiano-Reggiano, but a good, fresh, and moist piece of Padano can, on occasion, serve as an acceptable and less expensive alternative.

PECORINO ROMANO

Pecorino romano is not about nuances. It's about blunt power; it's the bite of sheep's milk cheese sharpened by salt. During its first weeks of maturation, it is rubbed with salt, at first every day, then at gradually broader intervals. It is ready for grating after a minimum of eight months, but the best cheese makers age it longer.

The impact of pecorino romano can excite the palate, and a well-made example is exactly the cheese you want to cap the robust flavors of such Roman classics as a carbonara or an amatriciana. The pasta dish that best showcases its appeal is *cacio e pepe*, sauced with only a mound of grated pecorino romano that you loosen with a little pasta water as you toss it, and which you blanket with an exceptionally liberal fresh grinding of black pepper.

The most devoted consumers of pecorino romano are Italian Americans, who account for more than 70 percent of Italy's production. I have an elderly Neapolitan neighbor here in Florida who, in his long life, has never dusted his pasta with gratings from another cheese but romano. When I came to the States in 1955, and I began to shop Little Italy's grocers for ingredients, it was rare to find any other kind of hard cheese.

The word *pecorino* derives from the Italian for sheep, *pecora*.

The domestication of sheep long antedates the Christian era, and so does the production of cheeses from ewe's milk. Indeed, pecorino romano is Italy's oldest cheese, evoking for us the pastoral image of flocks grazing ancient Rome's countryside. Roman legionnaires, when deployed to expand and police the empire, counted on having a piece of the cheese in their daily rations. Sheep continue to crop the grass of the region's hills, and a few Roman producers such as Fulvi or Brunelli are the best sources of carefully aged pecorino romano. Today, however, the pecorino you buy is often Roman only in name. Most of it comes from the island of Sardinia, whose production is better able to deliver the quantities that are sent to America.

Pecorino romano is molded into tall, narrow, cylindrical forms, usually coated black for export, and varying in height from ten to eighteen inches. A wedge coming from the center, with no part of the rind from the bottom or top of the wheel, is the moistest and most desirable piece. The color of the cheese is either a stark white or an exceedingly pale, faded straw hue. Romano's consistency is hard and compact. Do not buy it grated or grate it long in advance, because it will dry quickly. Bring a good piece home, wrap it tightly with a double layer of plastic wrap, then again with foil, and stow it in the refrigerator. It will keep for weeks. Rewrap it well after each time you use it.

Pecorino romano is a legally controlled name that applies solely to a cheese from central Italy, or the island of Sardinia, made with ewe's milk from particular breeds of sheep grazing on designated pasturage. Do not be misled by the name *romano* on American and Canadian cheeses, which are produced under loose regulations that do not even require them to be made from sheep's milk.

Ventresca tuna packed in olive oil

TUNA PACKED IN OLIVE OIL

Il Tonno Sott'Olio

In almost every one of its edible manifestations, whether eaten fresh or out of a can packed in water, tuna bores me. The one exception, when it achieves a miraculous transformation, one might even call it a transubstantiation, is tuna packed in olive oil in the Italian or Spanish manner. No food gives me greater pleasure. Whenever I open a tin of really good tuna in olive oil, it doesn't matter what I intend to do with its contents, I help myself to a preliminary nibble or two. Once I have removed the tuna from the can, I use a little fork to bring to my lips any fragment remaining in the tin.

What I often make with it is this classic Italian tuna salad: Slice a mild onion very thin. (In Italy we'd want to use the red torpedo-shaped Tropea onion; here one can choose any of the sweet onion varieties available, or else sweeten the onion by soaking it in water as described on page 76.) Spread freshly cooked, slightly warm cannellini or borlotti beans over the onion. Top with shards of high-quality canned tuna packed in olive oil. Toss with salt, red wine vinegar, and extra virgin olive oil. Accompany with good crusty bread.

I sometimes make a tuna spread that I serve to guests on tiny crostini before dinner or put on grilled slices of bread to take with me on a plane, along with other good things, as my alternative to airline food. Put canned tuna packed in olive oil in a food processor with butter (yes, butter), a mashed anchovy fillet, diced cornichons, and capers, and process to a smooth but still slightly chunky consistency. It is even better if, instead of using the food processor, you mash all the ingredients in a bowl with a fork.

Canned tuna packed in olive oil is what you want in a Niçoise salad, demonstrating that fresh is not always best.

There are many enjoyable ways to use canned tuna packed in olive oil in a pasta sauce. One that I particularly like combines tuna crumbled out of the can with roasted bell peppers, garlic, and capers.

The most ravishing thing you can do with good canned tuna is the sauce with mayonnaise, anchovies, and capers, in which you steep slices of cold, poached veal or pork, the elegant Italian contribution to a summer table, *vitello tonnato.*

Ventresca

The sweet, fatty, pale flesh of the tuna's belly is called *ventresca*—from the Italian *ventre*, for "belly"—a separate, expensive category of canned tuna. It corresponds to the raw

Japanese *toro*, highly sought after for sushi or sashimi. It can go, like regular tuna in olive oil, into salads and sauces, but it is almost too sweet, even bland, not to mention too costly, for such compound uses. It is best enjoyed on its own, out of hand, on the points of a fork, with a slice of buttered bread.

ANCHOVIES, CAPERS, CHILIS, SPICES, AND HERBS

Le Spezie e Gli Odori

Italian cooks make stingy use of spices and herbs, because the guiding principle of the country's regional cuisines is that the flavors of a dish should be the undisguised ones of its basic ingredients. The role of a spice or herb or other flavoring agent is that of an accent that prompts recognition of a familiar taste sensation, as rosemary does of roast chicken or sage of game, or at most it is that of a fanfare calling the palate to attention, which is what a little bit of chili pepper does in sautéed rapini.

ANCHOVIES

Le Acciughe o Alici

An ingredient that I, along with every good cook I have known, am most grateful for, is the anchovy. It has a self-effacing flavor that accommodates itself to any role you assign it. Mash it to a pulp and add it to a roasting veal shank, where it will divest itself of its explicit identity while adding depth to the flavor of the meat. Stir it into chopped garlic sautéing in olive oil, and you have the foundation of scores of lively sauces for pasta or vegetable dishes. It is indispensable in *bagna cauda*, the Piedmontese dip for raw vegetables, and in *salsa verde*, the piquant green sauce for poached fish or boiled brisket of beef. A fine, large, meaty, lustrous anchovy—not the cheap, salty, wizened ones packed in tiny cans—is fabulous on its own as a crostino, served on buttered bread, or with peeled, roasted peppers.

The best anchovies are the large ones that are packed in salt whole and sold by the piece. The grocer pries them loose, one by one, out of a big can. To prepare the fillets at home, I'd first rinse away the salt, then scrape off the skin, remove the dorsal fin, open them up, pull away the center bone, and separate each fish into two beautiful fillets that I'd lay flat on a shallow dish and cover with olive oil.

Unhappily, in recent years, I have been unable to find whole, large anchovies packed in salt and sold loose. There are anchovies packed in salt available in smaller cans for home cooks. I have tried them and found them mushy. I prefer high-quality fillets packed in olive oil by such companies as Ortiz, Scalia, or Recca.

Colatura di alici

Colatura Di Alici

The name—Italian for "anchovy drippings"—exactly describes the product, but *colatura* tastes much better than it sounds. Think of it as essence of anchovy. Fresh anchovies are salted, packed down flat in a wooden barrel, and heavily weighted. A light, golden liquid that the anchovies discharge flows out of an opening at the bottom of the barrel, where it is collected. *Colatura* descends from an ancient condiment that Romans called *garum*. Vietnamese fermented and odorous nuoc mam is a contemporary relation, but *colatura* is sleeker, fresher smelling.

The best use for *colatura* is with a pasta sauce based on garlic and olive oil, which may also include tomatoes and seafood. I don't cook the *colatura*; I swirl a heaping spoonful of it, or even a spoonful and a half if I am cooking for four or more, into the sauce with which I am tossing the pasta. It's heady. Use spaghetti or linguine only, no fettuccine or other egg pasta.

Colatura di alici is a specialty of a town called Cetara, in Campania, and its preeminent bottler is Nettuno.

CAPERS

I Capperi

Capers, the hand-harvested flower buds of the Mediterranean caper bush, need something soft in which to sink their bite. It could be the softness of the tuna and mayonnaise sauce for *vitello tonnato*. The sponginess of a Neapolitan pizza. The mildness of sautéed swordfish, or pork. How bland would a puttanesca taste without capers! I must always have them on fine smoked salmon.

Capers have a lovely aroma that is smothered by the vinegar in which they are customarily pickled. The best capers, such as those growing on the volcanic islands of Salina and Pantelleria, off Sicily, are packed in salt. Rinse the salt away before using them, and then enjoy their clear, spirited flavor without the distractions of a pickling vinegar. If you rinse

more capers than you can use, store the excess in a little jar, cover them with olive oil, and refrigerate.

There are small capers called nonpareils, "without equals," and large capers, which usually come from one of the Italian islands. I prefer the full, robust flavor of the large Italian capers.

CHILI PEPPER

Il Peperoncino

The chili pepper used in some of the dishes of central and southern Italy, of which the best-known, no doubt, is spaghetti *aglio, olio e peperoncino*, is a slim, horn-shaped, approximately two-inch-long, spicy red pepper popularly known as *diavolicchio*, or "little devil." It measures just 30,000 Scoville units, so it is not too devilish. Pleasant aromas temper its moderate fire.

Peperoncino is sold fresh or dried, loose or in bunches, whole or ground or powdered. I prefer it dried and whole, which allows me to mince as much as I want of the spicy part, the pod.

The most flavorful peperoncino comes from Calabria. You can buy it online from Alma Gourmet and other sites that specialize in Italian products.

Out of a desire for variety, I sometimes use jalapeños. I like the exotic accent of their aroma, which harmonizes successfully with some of my sauces and meat braises. With sautéed vegetables in the Apulian style however, I stick to Calabrian *diavolicchio*. As a backup, for those occasions that I run out of peperoncino, I keep a supply of dried *aji panca*, a Peruvian chili.

Spaghetti *aio e oio*, with garlic, olive oil, and chili pepper, is a dish demonstrating that, in Italian cooking, simple

Chili peppers

doesn't necessarily mean easy. Outside of Rome, I have rarely, if ever, had a perfectly seasoned *aio e oio*. One of the defects is that often the garlic is burnt. I mince it very fine, put it in the pan at the same time as the oil, and sauté it at medium heat together with the chili pepper until it slowly becomes colored a deep, tawny gold. Another problem is that the finished dish is often shy of salt. You cannot add it to the sauce because salt won't dissolve in olive oil. Before draining the pasta, I save some of its water, and as I toss the spaghetti in the pan, I add a tablespoon or so of salty pasta water. I sometimes skip cooking the sauce. I steep raw minced garlic and ground chili pepper with an intense extra virgin olive oil in a warm covered bowl for thirty minutes to an hour. Toss with drained, hot, fully cooked spaghetti, some pasta water, and it's done.

BLACK PEPPER

Il Pepe

In Italian cooking, the color of pepper is black. A black peppercorn is a small, dried fruit whose wrinkled skin surrounds a white core. There are aromatic substances held by the peppercorn's black outer layer that release floral and citrusy scents, distantly evocative of thyme, marjoram, rosemary, and cedar. It is the promise of these aromas, traveling on gentle waves of heat, that has rewarded black pepper with universal employment. Pepper is present on an extraordinary variety of Italian foods, brightening the taste of soups, broths, salumi, and grilled and braised meats of all kinds. A few fine, freshly ground grains of pepper bring uplift to buffalo mozzarella, burrata, or a slice of Tuscan pecorino. Without black pepper, a host of Roman pasta dishes, *cacio e pepe, alla gricia*, and amatriciana among them, would not exist. At the same time, in the north, it freshens the meat fillings of homemade pasta dumplings.

South America and Asia are the main sources of black pepper. The best, surpassing all others, comes from Tellicherry, in India. It is a large and comparatively heavy, dark berry, moderate in heat, but fresher in taste and with a more complex aroma than any other pepper.

You should buy only whole peppercorns. Throw out any powdered pepper you may have been keeping on your shelf or in a shaker. Store your peppercorns in a tightly closed jar. Grind the pepper no more in advance than the time you need it; soon after grinding the most desirable of its aromas begin to fade. White peppercorns are black peppercorns stripped of their skins, and consequently stripped of much of their aromatic quality.

NUTMEG, MACE, ALLSPICE

La Noce Moscata, Il Macis, Il Pimento

Nutmeg's finest moment is, I believe, in the final aromatic touch it brings to *ragù*, Bolognese meat sauce. Without it, the meat sauce is unfinished, but too much of it, and the *ragù* is spoiled. Judicious use of nutmeg is a wonderful thing—it bestows an exotic warmth and sweetness to meats and sauces, but an excess leaves an ineradicable mark of bitterness.

In addition to its place in a *ragù*, Italian cooks grate a little nutmeg into the fillings of pasta dumplings, into mashed potatoes, and into the béchamel sauce of vegetable gratins. Some use it in braises and stews because nutmeg can certainly flatter a meat dish, but I do it with great circumspection to avoid that taint of bitterness.

It is useless to buy grated nutmeg. You must grate it fresh. A cylindrical Microplane grater does the job perfectly for me. Store whole nutmeg in a tightly closed jar, and discard the nut when it has been ground down to a nub.

Mace is the nutmeg's orange cloak. It is considerably milder than the nut itself. It can be ground in a food processor or with a pestle in a mortar and used as one would nutmeg with shyer results. Some exploit its orange hue by adding it to pasta dough to give it a warmer color.

Nutmeg is the seed of its tree, native to Indonesia. Allspice is a berry from a plant that grows in Central America. Although botanically and geographically distant, they share, to a surprising degree, a similar aroma. Allspice is sweeter than nutmeg, and I am not apprehensive when I grate it over pasta with a cream sauce, because I know it is safe and good to do so.

Buy only whole allspice, not powdered. Store it in a tightly closed glass container. To grind it, use a pepper grinder.

FLAT-LEAF PARSLEY

Il Prezzemolo

There are two dozen or more varieties of parsley, but the only one we use in Italian cooking is the flat-leaf version, because it has the most flavor. It is used to contribute to the flavor foundation of innumerable dishes: in braises, soups, some tomato sauces, seafood (*linguine con le vongole*), meats (think of thin chicken breasts Siena style with just parsley and lemon juice or *veal scaloppine al limone*), and in the combination of olive oil, garlic, and parsley that constitutes the classic medium for sautéing mushrooms. Parsley is so diffuse in Italy that we say of someone whom we are continually running into, *"Sei come il prezzemolo."* (You're like parsley.) It's an observation that would have more currency in Old World cities and towns, where people move on foot and acquaintances do indeed bump into one another.

Both the leaves and the stems of flat-leaf parsley have flavor, but the one of the leaves is much more pronounced than that of the stems. The leaves can be minced very fine or chopped coarsely. It is done better with a sharp chef's knife, but if you have a large quantity to prepare, a food processor does an acceptable job. Parsley leaves must be dry before mincing or processing. If they are moist, press them firmly between sheets of paper towels. The stems are used whole in meat braises such as osso buco or when making broth. If they are in a meat dish, remove them before serving.

Buy parsley whose leaves are vivid green with no sign of yellowing or wilting. At home, wrap the stem half of a bunch of parsley in a wet paper towel, put the bunch in a plastic bag, and store in the vegetable drawer, where it will keep easily for a week.

If you are about to mince parsley that has begun to wilt in the refrigerator, detach the leaves from the stems, put them in a bowl of ice water for ten to fifteen minutes, and they will revive. Spin off all the water clinging to them and squeeze them dry between paper towels before mincing. If you should have a quantity of minced leaves left over, refrigerate them in an airtight plastic bag. They will keep for three or four days. Do not ever use dried parsley, which is tasteless.

Rosemary

ROSEMARY

Il Rosmarino

You are an Italian child coming home from school. You are greeted by the distinct scent of rosemary coming from the kitchen, and you may confidently assume that what you will be having for dinner is a roast—any kind of roasted meat, veal, pork, chicken, lamb, rabbit. The saliva-quickening pungency that rosemary broadcasts while it cooks is the default accompaniment of nearly every meat roast cooked in the Italian manner, on top of the stove.

Rosemary is the most desirable partner for chickpeas both in soups and in a sauté; for potatoes, particularly when roasted in lard; for *pasta e fagioli*. It is insuperable in a focaccia-style flat bread, and sometimes I chop the leaves very fine, to a powder—it must be done with a knife—and sprinkle them on a loaf of bread I am reheating in the oven.

In Italy, rosemary grows so abundantly wild that it is only city dwellers who need to buy it. I must buy it, too, in Florida. Strangely, it is the only herb that doesn't flourish here, on my Gulf-side terrace. I buy potted plants of rosemary and must replace them periodically. If you are buying cut sprigs—never buy powdered, dried rosemary—choose ones that are soft, not woody. The color of the green leaves should be bright, and they must be firmly attached to the branch, not coming loose easily. Smell it; the fragrance should be strong and clear.

Sage

SAGE

La Salvia

The fragrance of the soft, furry, gray-green leaves of fresh sage, an extremely easy plant to grow in a window box, is teasingly penetrating. It is the traditional herb to use with game, and its presence is prominent in any home where there is a hunter. I no longer get to cook game, but I use scaloppine and sage to make the classic Venetian dish *osei scampai*—"flown birds" made of veal. Meat stews braised with sage and mushrooms, wild mushrooms preferably, are pleasingly redolent of the rich fragrances of game cookery.

I consider sage indispensable for cooking dried beans, especially cannellini and cranberry beans. I cook the soaked, drained beans in olive oil and water, peeled crushed garlic, and as many fresh sage leaves as I can bring myself to pluck from my plant.

Another good thing to do with very fresh sage is to fry it, dipping each leaf separately in *pastella*, a light flour and water batter. The combination with fried squash blossoms can be sublime.

When fresh sage leaves are not available, dried leaves are convenient to have, but not for frying. Follow the same advice I've been giving with other herbs; do not buy them in powdered form.

THYME

Il Timo

Thyme is the elegant herb. There is a fine edge to its fragrance, which is suave, cool, and penetrating. I seek occasions to use thyme, and the best one is usually with seafood. My favorite example is the large, deep-sea scallops prepared as we do in Venice. First salt the scallops, then add a few drops of lemon juice followed by a generous cover of thyme leaves patiently stripped from the stems, top with bread crumbs, and drizzle lightly with olive oil. Bake in a very hot oven for five to six minutes. You'll need bread because there will be marvelous juices to sop up.

Thyme is an ideal match for sautéed zucchini, and I also use it in a sauce of young fava beans and guanciale or pancetta that I make for pasta. Thyme elevates the tone of a vegetable frittata, particularly if it is fresh. Use it also in minestrone and with meat stews. It's lovely with lamb.

I have found thyme an easy plant to cultivate both here in Florida, and in Venice where I once lived. A pot of it can thrive on a balcony or in a window box. Thyme is most appealing when clipped fresh from the plant, but if it has been properly dried, it maintains most of its fragrance. I try to always have on hand dried whole thyme stems imported from Sicily in a cellophane bag. It is available online and in some of the stores that specialize in Italian foods. The package makes it very easy to separate the leaves from the stems, which can otherwise be a chore. I shake and squeeze the closed bag and retrieve from it the leaves that drop off the sprigs.

Do not use powdered thyme. Farmers' markets usually have a stand that sells herbs, and there you may find sprigs of fresh or dried thyme. Supermarkets sell fresh sprigs packaged in plastic. Sometimes they are fine, but their shelf life is short. Make sure their color has not dulled, and open the package and sniff to make sure the fragrance is still lively. If you buy sprigs of fresh thyme, keep them no longer than a week, refrigerated in a tightly closed plastic bag.

OREGANO AND MARJORAM

L'Origano e La Maggiorana

Oregano speaks dialect; it is eloquent in a vigorous expression of the exuberant flavors of southern Italian food. It receives its friendliest welcome in tomatoes: raw tomatoes in a salad, tomatoes saucing pasta or braising a chicken fricassee or a lamb stew, in clams or mussels with tomatoes. Oregano's most popular performance may be in partnering tomatoes and mozzarella in pizza Margherita. Oregano and lemon are also a brilliant duet as in *salmoriglio*, the matchless sauce for swordfish. Sprinkle it on grilled eggplants, peppers, and zucchini. If you pickle vegetables, its aroma is well-suited to eggplants, artichokes, mushrooms, and peppers.

Fresh oregano is very much milder than the dried, which is what you will choose if you seek its full-throated fragrance. Dried oregano keeps a long while in a tightly closed glass container. I buy the whole twigs, which are imported from Italy or Greece, packaged in cellophane. I shake off or rub loose the leaves.

Marjoram comes from a different branch of the oregano family. Its fragrance is gentler than oregano's; it makes one think of a mild version of thyme. Drying silences marjoram's delicate fragrance; fresh is the only useful way to have it.

Marjoram is closely linked to the cooking of the Riviera, in northwestern Italy. It goes into the ground meat mixture of that cuisine's celebrated filled vegetables, *i ripieni*. It is used freely in soups, on pan-roasted fish, on shellfish and crustaceans with fresh tomatoes, over vegetable frittatas. Marjoram's fragrance is charming but fragile; it does not survive long cooking.

It grows well in a window box or small balcony, and it ought to be clipped from the plant just before cooking.

BAY LEAVES

L'Alloro

Should I encourage you to use bay leaves? Certainly. Their tealike aroma makes a valuable contribution to long-cooked dishes such as soups, meat broths, stews, boiled potatoes, braised artichokes, steamed fish, or if packed with pickled vegetables. Should you prefer dried to fresh? Once again, certainly. Unlike most herbs whose fragrance dissipates when they are dried, that of the bay leaf, like that of oregano, emerges when drying concentrates and refines it. In this country, moreover, it is prudent to buy imported dried leaves coming from the desirable Mediterranean laurel plant rather than the leaves of the California bay laurel, often sold fresh, which have a strong medicinal accent of eucalyptol.

The sharpness of a dry bay leaf can cause internal damage if it is swallowed, hence it should be carefully picked out and removed after cooking. If you break up the leaves to enhance the release of their fragrance, wrap them in muslin so that they can be safely removed before serving the dish.

Store whole dry bay leaves in a tightly closed glass jar. If you haven't used them all after a year, discard and replace them.

In Italian, the herb is called *alloro* (laurel) after its parent plant, *Laurus nobilis.* Laurel is a name with magnificent resonance. In Greek mythology, the plant was considered divine, a symbol of honor, wisdom, and glory. A circlet of it crowned the head of the winner of the Delphic Games and, as acknowledgment of the highest honors, the head of a distinguished poet. To this day, our country bestows a similar honor when it designates a poet as laureate. A university degree in Italy is called a *laurea*, and a graduate a *laureato* or, in my case, a *laureata*. I don't understand why the leaf is called "bay" instead of "laurel," why it has exchanged the glorious symbolism of its history in favor of such a modest and unsung appellation.

Basil

SWEET BASIL

Il Basilico

Small-leaved sweet basil, sometimes known as Genovese, is the superstar of Italian herbs. It is irresistible on ripe tomatoes, in salads, scattered on a pizza Margherita after it comes out of the oven, and most famously in pesto. From the list, one quickly infers that it is meant to be used raw. Indeed, all the charm of basil—its cheerful hue, its effusive clove-like and minty scent, all its notable properties—vanish when heated. In a caprese it is irreplaceable; cooked it is almost useless.

Basil grows so easily in a sunny spot that you should make every effort to take your basil leaves from a living plant. Packaged fresh basil, its leaves preferably small, can take the place of the real thing, when there is no alternative. Do not keep it any longer than the day you buy it. I have known of, and tried, various methods of keeping cut basil leaves, including freezing. I am not satisfied that any of them supplies what I am eager for when I use basil.

The whole leaf looks immensely attractive with sliced tomatoes or on a caprese, but it will release more fragrance if you tear it first.

Thai and other Asian basils are not fully successful as substitutes for sweet basil in Italian salads, and certainly not in pesto.

BORAGE

La Boraggine

There is a small town called Sori roosting above the rocky shore of the Italian Riviera, about twelve miles south of Genoa. My husband and I once spent a summer in Sori, where I became acquainted with borage, a wild, luxuriant, green herb with spectacular, star-shaped violet-blue flowers. The leaves are covered by a pale hairy fuzz, bristly in the larger leaves, almost velvety in the younger, smaller ones, which are used in the fragrant cooking of several of the Riviera's dishes. The most popular employment for borage is in the filling of *pansoti*, famous herb and cheese ravioli triangles served with a walnut sauce. To prepare the filling, you assemble an assortment of borage and other wild herbs, blanch them, chop them up, and mix them with an egg, Parmesan, some nutmeg, and a local yogurt-like fresh cheese called *prescinseua*. The sauce on *pansoti* is an emulsion of walnuts, milk, soft bread crumbs, Parmesan, pine nuts, garlic, and olive oil.

Borage has a cool, mildly sour, and pleasant taste that makes one think of cucumber. You can blanch and chop a mixture of fresh borage and wild herbs, such as is used in the filling of *pansoti*, and stir it into a minestrone. A borage frittata can be formidably delicious.

I have read recently that borage can be added raw to salads. There seem to be few things that people in the States won't put in a salad. However, every cook I spoke to when I was in Sori emphatically warned me not to eat borage raw. It's toxic, they said, if it is not thoroughly cooked.

JUNIPER BERRIES

Le Bacche di Ginepro

Juniper berries are not berries at all, but the tiny, tightly closed seed cones of the juniper bush. Their unique resinous scent—I believe it is the only spice of conifer origin in Western cooking—is fresh and agreeably tart, with a citrusy accent. It emerges best in slow, gentle cooking when it is in contact with lamb or game birds or hare or venison. Crush the berries lightly to give their flavors a lift, but don't pulverize them.

There is a lamb shoulder that I roast over the stove—a farmhouse recipe from Lombardy, in northern Italy—to which juniper berries make a significant contribution. I omit, for once, the conventional preliminary browning and put everything into the pot at the same time: the cut-up shoulder, vegetables, garlic, rosemary, wine, and the wonderful piney and citrusy crushed juniper berries. The contents of the pot look discouragingly gray in its early stages, but after three hours or so of carefully monitored slow cooking, they become a glorious deep brown, the meat subtly infused with juniper aromas.

MINT

La Menta

Mint may grow faster than an epidemic, but it doesn't reach many Italian kitchens. Roman cooks are the ones who make great use of it. Mint is essential to *carciofi alla romana*, artichokes braised in olive oil, cooked and served upside down with their long stems attached. A mixture of mint, parsley, garlic, and ground black pepper fills the vegetable's cavity. Before cooking, the tough tops of the artichoke's leaves are trimmed away and the stem peeled to render the vegetable tender and exquisitely edible in all its parts. Mint is also used with tripe, one of the most popular of the city's traditional dishes.

I don't know of other significant uses of mint in everyday Italian cooking, but in the Veneto, where I lived for many years, it is used with *frutti di bosco* (small, wild berries). When it is the season for foragers to come to the market with red and white currants, blueberries, raspberries, blackberries, tiny *fragoline* (wood strawberries), we collect as wide an assortment as we can, wash the fruit, and put it in a bowl with sugar, a few drops of lemon juice, and torn-up mint leaves.

Whether you use mint cooked or raw, use only fresh leaves plucked as recently as possible from the plant. The mint family is packed with many different members. In Italy, one would not use anything as aggressive as peppermint, known as *menta piperita*. The fragrance of the mint used in Rome, popularly called *mentuccia*, is cool, but mild.

RED WINE VINEGAR

L'Aceto di Vino Rosso

There was a restaurant in Sarasota where they kept two special bottles for me at the bar. One was for my after-dinner bourbon tipple; the other was a very good red wine vinegar. When you are eating out, it is discouraging to ask for olive oil and vinegar with which to toss your own salad and have the waiter bring balsamic with the oil. "No, not balsamic! Please bring red wine vinegar." "Sorry, ma'am, balsamic is all we have." What a calamity. Why make a salad taste sweet? I have also heard from chefs who tell me they send out their salads tossed with only olive oil and salt, I assumed to accommodate those who want to drink wine with salad. Flat, nerveless salads. How boring.

Someday I hope to see good red wine vinegar restored to its long-honored place, alongside extra virgin olive oil and sea salt, as one of the three essential condiments of a salad. I would also hope we might be weaned from the vinaigrette habit that weighs upon the immediacy, the refreshing lightness of good greens. The fragrance in a few round drops of a really good red wine vinegar is sufficient to brighten the flavor of any salad, whether it is composed of mixed small field greens, or boiled, peeled potatoes, or tuna, onion, and beans, or an elaborate Niçoise. My husband and I like a small dab of vinegar on a caprese; it draws out the sappiness of the tomato, making it taste sweeter and riper.

When the wine making process moves forward without interruption, vinegar is its conclusion. Acetic acid bacteria takes up where alcoholic fermentation stopped, converting wine's alcohol into vinegar's acid. There are two approaches to the making of vinegar. The modern, most commonly used approach, takes only a few hours. Wine, together with a glob of acetic acid bacteria, known more affectionately as the mother, fill a stainless steel or aluminum tank. Rapidly circulated oxygen increases the mother's alcohol-devouring bacteria, which quickly turns the alcohol into acetic acid. The wine becomes vinegar in less than a day. It is quite possible to make good vinegar by this accelerated method, depending on the quality of the wine. Some producers age the vinegar afterward for a year or more in barrels.

A slower process, developed centuries ago, is the Orléans method. An active vinegar mother is introduced into an oak barrel of wine. There is no forced circulation of oxygen to stimulate the mother's growth, and its bacteria will convert the wine's alcohol into acetic acid at a natural, slow pace. It may take up to three months, instead of the alternate method's half day. When the vinegar is ready, it is drawn off and replaced by a fresh supply of wine. The Orléans method presumably delivers more of the wine's aroma and nuance. It always depends, of course, on the choice of wine. A hard, tannic wine may not yield the freshness and fruitiness one hopes for in vinegar.

An unopened bottle of vinegar is said to last indefinitely. I can't say and I wonder how anyone else might know. I buy a case at a time containing twelve bottles of excellent vinegar made from Valpolicella red grape varieties—a vinegar my son bottles and imports—and several months later, the last bottle from the case that I open is still in mint condition. I store an open bottle in the refrigerator. It not only preserves it, but the refrigerator's cold temperature causes any solid matter to drop to the bottom of the bottle, leaving the vinegar clear and bright.

I prefer the roundness of red wine, its fruitiness and berry freshness, as the source of vinegar, but I have also used sherry vinegar. I don't dislike it; the flavor is rich, but sherry lacks the vibrancy, the fragrant youthfulness of red wine, and sometimes sherry may have an undesirably sweet touch. I don't use infused vinegars or vinegars made from anything but wine from grapes.

BUTTER AND LARD

Il Burro e Lo Strutto

I come from Italy's cow and pig country, Emilia Romagna, and butter and home-rendered lard were familiar presences in my mother's kitchen. Nor did we ever lack excellent fresh olive oil, which came from my uncles' farms, either in the hills of Romagna or on the shore of Lake Garda. Not many days pass in my kitchen without my using olive oil. It is the very soul of my Mediterranean culinary heritage, but in the cooking traditions of my country, there are other seas besides the Mediterranean. There is Liguria's Tyrrhenian; there is the northern Adriatic of my native Romagna.

Butter has a legitimate place in the everyday cooking of Italy's northern regions, as well as in some of the celebratory holiday specialties of the south. I would not want to be without its luxurious smoothness, its roundness, the full taste it elicits from any preparation of which it is part. I won't have some of my pasta sauces diminished by its absence. A swirl of unsalted butter can also be a successful corrective for a soup or a sauce that tastes a little saltier than you would have liked.

When we lived in Milan, we often spent a long weekend in Liguria, Italy's Riviera, exchanging numb, colorless March days in town for Liguria's sunny hillsides and flower-decked windows. We made good friends, one of whom, the Marquis Giuseppe Gavotti, eventually became secretary general of L'Accademia Italiana della Cucina, a rather tony epicurean society whose charter excluded professionals. With Gavotti we talked of little else but food, particularly of the traditional dishes that graced his table. It was Gavotti who taught me to add a little butter to pesto. "It's the way they do it in all the old families," he said. "Other people don't do it because butter is too expensive." That is the way I published the recipe in my first book, and notwithstanding the accusations of heresy, I have never been tempted to do it differently.

From pesto and other regional sauces that are never cooked, such as the Sicilian *salmoriglio*, I have spun off a series of raw sauces that work particularly well on fish. One of them is a summery emulsion of basil, chopped onion, salt, lemon juice, olive oil, and butter that I usually serve with baked salmon. At other, cooler times, I omit the basil and onion and make the sauce with thyme—my favorite herb for fish—a touch of mustard, lemon juice, olive oil, and again, butter.

There has been much talk recently of cultured butter in the European style. Actually, before pasteurization, it was once the prevailing style in America as well. Milk collected in the evening was left to settle during the cooler night hours, giving the cream time to rise. The microorganisms present capitalized on the lack of refrigeration to develop and produce agreeably cheesy flavors in the milk and its cream. The butter churned from that cream might have resembled the tangy and nutty butter that we now describe as cultured. When pasteurization came, Americans found, not unreasonably, that they preferred the new sweet cream butter. Europeans instead chose live cultures to put back into the cream and recapture the taste of the butter they had been used to.

The percentage of fat is also a frequent subject of interest. The minimum the FDA requires is 80 percent butterfat. It might seem obvious to assume that the richer in butterfat and denser the butter, the more useful it would be. This is not always true. I have tried butters that were very high in butterfat, such as the Straus Family line, but I did not like the effect they had on the taste of a sauce I was making. The high butterfat dominated the lighter aromas in the sauce.

One of the butters that harmonizes well with my cooking is Land O'Lakes. I also like the Vermont Creamery's version of European cultured butter. Among the European butters, I enjoy the lushness of Ireland's Kerrygold and the finesse of several Breton Baratte butters. I wish I could find Beppino Occelli's extraordinary cultured mountain butter from Piedmont. It was once briefly available online; then it disappeared.

If I may voice a feeling of mild annoyance, I wish recipe writers would stop specifying unsalted butter. If it isn't to be used in baking, whether it is salted or not is none of their business. It is up to the cook to decide. Moreover, the aromas of butter are sensitive to the conditions of its storage. Salt protects them from undesirable influences. I have on a few occasions found that the unsalted butter I had brought home had off odors. Salted butter would have been fresher.

Lard

What lard can do, it does better than any other cooking fat. Lard envelops fried foods with the crispest, most delicate coating, it makes the best biscuits and the flakiest piecrusts, and when it is done, it disappears, leaving behind no odor, no grease, no taste of itself. No other cooking medium behaves with such refinement.

The lard I am describing is not the package that you find in a store on an unrefrigerated shelf. That is hydrogenated trans fat, just as some vegetable shortenings are trans fats because they have been hydrogenated to make them solid and long-lived at room temperature. The lard I speak of is pure pork fat, melted at slow heat and allowed to harden naturally, unaltered by any other process, free of all preservatives. It can be stored at moderate room temperature for up to twenty days, or refrigerated for three or four months. It can also be frozen, but you should use it within a year.

Lard was once a boon to poor families, who had easy access to abundant raw pork fat and melted it themselves at low heat. My mother made excellent lard from rendered—melted—pork fat. Making it at home yields a bonus—the delightfully crunchy, tasty solid bits that reward you when you strain the melted fat through fine cheesecloth. They are cracklings, *ciccioli* in Italian. The choicest fat for making lard is that surrounding the kidneys, known as the leaf. The next choicest is back fat, and then comes the belly fat. It takes several hours to render fat on a home stove, but if you grind the fat first it will go faster.

I am loath to talk about chemical properties of food, but you may more easily be persuaded to try non-hydrogenated pure lard if I tell you that it has a high level of the "good fat," monounsaturated fat, and a relatively low level of saturated fat, 20 percent less than butter. It has a high percentage of vitamin D, which vegetable oils lack, and it has a much higher smoke point than butter.

You can find sources of non-hydrogenated lard online. Unfortunately, what was once a resource for poor families has become very expensive, costing as much as eighteen dollars a pound for the best leaf lard. And even more unhappily, a little lard does not go a long way. A large dollop of it vanishes quickly in cooking.

BREAD CRUMBS

Il Pangrattato

If you don't own a food processor, making bread crumbs at home could be a plausible motive for getting one. Good bread crumbs are immensely useful, and the only way to have them is to produce your own. Boxed bread crumbs from the store, even those deceptively labeled "plain," all contain ingredients and flavorings added to grated bread that you want to keep out of careful home cooking.

The most familiar example of how bread crumbs are used in Italian cooking may be in the breading of meat cutlets—veal, chicken, or pork—in the Milanese style. Use them also to bread meatballs, and when you brown pieces of meat or vegetables such as artichoke wedges. Crumbs absorb moisture, favoring crispness.

Bread crumbs are essential to the marinade that I use on all the fish that I either grill or bake. First I salt the fish, then sprinkle lemon juice and thoroughly coat the fillets with bread crumbs, which I finally moisten with a thin stream of olive oil. I now prefer to cook fish unsauced save for this marinade. I then make pesto-like sauces that I serve raw over the cooked fish.

In southern Italian cooking, we sometimes sprinkle bread

crumbs on pasta after we have tossed it. On pasta that has a runny, olive oil sauce, they bestow a fine, light-handed texture. Bread crumbs are well-suited to seafood pasta, in which they take the place of cheese.

To achieve the light, crackling texture that Italian cooks strive for, you need fine, dry bread crumbs, not soft and fresh. Nor do I find that panko, the Japanese bread crumb, which is otherwise an excellent product, is satisfactory in Italian cooking. To make my bread crumbs, I collect leftover bread—crusty, plain white bread, such as the excellent ciabatta that we use at table—and fill a brown paper bag with it. When it is dry, I break large pieces into small ones and grind it all in the food processor, as fine as it will come. I pass the ground crumbs through a fine-mesh strainer to eliminate the thicker crumbs. I store bread crumbs in the refrigerator in a large glass jar with a tightly closed cap. They last a very long time.

CROUTONS

Croutons—*crostini* in Italian—greatly magnify the pleasure of having soup. They are easy to prepare, and if you make them in quantity and freeze them, they will be ready to use whenever you want some.

I once used corn bread and enjoyed the croutons from it but I still prefer high-quality, plain, thick-sliced white bread. Trim away the crust and cut each slice into ¾-inch squares.

Fry them at medium heat, using any fat you prefer, spreading the cubes of bread, a batch at a time, in a single layer in a skillet. Butter or olive oil will each endow the croutons with its own distinctive flavor. Non-hydrogenated lard, which leaves no flavor, makes the crispest, lightest croutons. Fry over medium heat, carefully watching the bread squares in the pan and turning them quickly as soon as one side becomes colored a light gold. Cook the other side to the same hue, retrieve them from the pan using a slotted spatula, and let them drain on a cooling rack or on paper towels lining a dinner plate. If you are not using them right away, let the croutons cool completely, put them in resealable plastic bags, and freeze them.

SALT

Il Sale

Sea salt, rock salt, pink salt, gray salt, kosher salt, hand-harvested salt—the choices on offer for what is the most common ingredient we use in cooking are bewildering in their variety. It may be another manic food fad, but even if it is, I welcome it as long as it encourages us to turn to salt with the attention and respect it deserves. Using salt correctly and confidently is the most important skill a cook develops. Salt reaches deep into the ingredients of our dishes and draws from them aromas and flavors that would otherwise lie dormant. In Italian, food that lacks salt is described as *sciocco*, or "foolish."

When the ancient oceans evaporated, they left behind immense deposits of rock salt that we mine for our table and for industrial purposes. We also search for salt in the living waters of our seas and oceans, or large salty lakes, or salt-rich ponds. The flavors of sea salt harvested by evaporation are enriched by the trace minerals of its sources.

Salts I Have Used

- **Table Salt.** Table salt is rock salt crushed, made granular, given cubical shape, and purified. Unless it's been iodized—I have never been able to judge iodized salt correctly—ordinary table salt or kosher salt is what I add to pasta water. Using expensive sea salt for this purpose would be both extravagant and futile, because all its nuances would be lost.

- **Kosher Salt.** Like table salt, it is rock salt, but it is produced by methods that transform it into flakes rather than grains. The Diamond Crystal version of kosher salt is made by a patented process called Alberger that creates hollow, inverted cup-shaped crystals. As Shirley Corriher describes in *CookWise*, the difference between the granular cubes of table salt and the flakes of Diamond Crystal kosher salt is that between an ice cube and a snowflake. The flake adheres better to food and dissolves in half the time. To make Morton kosher salt, steel rollers are used to press granular salt into flakes. A tablespoon of Morton kosher salt has less salt than a tablespoon of table salt, but more salt than Diamond Crystal. Diamond Crystal kosher salt is a good product for a cook who has not yet achieved full confidence in her salting skills. It leaves a margin for error and provides the opportunity to learn to salt by pinches rather than by measuring spoons.

- **Gray Salt,** *Sel Gris.* This is a salt you might consider moving up to, once you have graduated from Diamond Crystal kosher salt. It is both an all-around cooking salt that bestows the flavor of its minerals on any food in the pot, and one that brings satisfying completion to the salad at the table. It is moderately coarse and it is moist, raked by hand after it has collected on the bottom of salt ponds.

- **Extra Fine Gray Salt.** A powdery form of *sel gris* that I use when I am making pesto or another raw sauce in which I want the salt to dissolve thoroughly and instantly. It would probably be very useful in baking, but you'd have to ask a baker.

- *Fleur de Sel, Fior di Sale.* In the shallow salt ponds of France, of Spain, of Portugal, of Greece, of Italy, when the sun beams and warm winds blow, water evaporates and fine salt crystals rise to sparkle on the surface. Patient men with hand rakes wait there to gather them before they sink. This is the most subtle and complex of salts; food's deepest flavors blossom at its contact. Île de Ré, Guérande, Camargue, and Noirmoutier are the place names on the Breton coast where French *fleur de sel* blooms. In Italy, there are impeccable salt flats off the northern coast of the Adriatic that I have passed thousands of times in my life. They are in Cervia, the town immediately next to mine. They call their salt *dolce* (sweet) because of its tender, warm, ripe touch on the palate. Another fine *fior di sale* from Italy is the one from Trapani, in Sicily; it is richly mineral, yet not so salty a salt.

- **Ravida.** A hefty salt from Sicily that I associate somehow with picnics at sea.

- **Maldon.** I love this English salt; I love to dispense it on a salad by crumbling its beautiful flakes between my fingers. It is a good salt, lacking most of salt's natural bitter back taste. It is complementary to all foods, but terrific on any that is fried, such as potatoes or shrimp or calamari.

- **Jacobsen.** Mr. Jacobsen produces beautiful, glittering crystal flakes from what he calls Oregon's cold waters. There is nothing cold about the salt; it is bold and strong, too bold perhaps for general cooking, but quite dynamic as a finishing salt.

- **Himalayan Pink Salt.** This salt, as delightful in appearance as it is in taste, is chipped off an immense salt mountain in Pakistan. It is sold both coarse and ground fine. I use the finely ground version when I need quick integration into a dish.

- **Amabito no Moshio.** Recently, a friend brought a small packet from Japan containing cream-colored grains as fine as powder-soft sand. No other salt has such suave manners. It disappears into the food you sprinkle it on—I used it on briefly cooked king salmon—and flavors emerge with precision and clarity.

Before you make a lasting commitment to the use of any salt, taste a few. The effect of salt on the taste of tomatoes can be dramatically clear. Take one or two firm, ripe Roma tomatoes, slice them crosswise into rounds, and use one round for each salt that you are tasting. On one or two rounds sprinkle table salt or kosher salt as a foil.

The good cook's way to measure salt is by pinches. When you distribute salt that you hold between the tips of thumb and forefinger, or even adding the middle finger, you acquire an enjoyable tactile sense of the texture and volume of the grains and flakes of your salt, and you come to understand exactly how much you are using. You don't need to use all the salt you are holding; if you have some left after you have used what you feel is enough, return the remainder to the salt pig. When you use your fingers, you are better able to distribute salt evenly. Hold your hand high above the dish or pan or raw ingredient that you are salting and move the hand around while you rub your fingertips, causing the salt to sprinkle like rain over the whole surface of the food you are seasoning.

TOMATO PASTE

Il Concentrato di Pomodoro

On my desk there are two cans, two tubes, and one glass jar of tomato paste. The cans are from California. One of them is Contadina, the only brand I found when, in 1955, I arrived from Italy. Its label lists twenty ingredients, in addition to tomato. The sauce from that can is a dark, somber red. It tastes strong, sour, and spiced, like cheap pizza. In the back of the mouth, it is faintly bitter. The other canned tomato paste from California is Muir Glen. Its list has just two ingredients, tomato and citric acid. The color is a bright red, the taste, mild, fresh, tomatoey.

The paste in the tubes is imported from Italy. One brand is Amore; the other has appropriated the San Marzano name. Both list just one ingredient, tomato. Both are labeled "double concentrated." The Italian food authority defines three degrees of concentration, of which "double" is the mid-level and most broadly available and in which a little more than thirteen pounds of tomatoes are reduced and concentrated to slightly less than two pounds of paste. The tomatoes are chopped, heated, and strained, and the filtered juice is gradually reduced by evaporation in an industrial concentrator.

The paste that squeezes softly from the tube is bright red. It has a pleasant, vigorous taste of tomato.

The jar is labeled *estratto*. It is produced in Sicily, where it is called *strattu*. My sample comes from Pianogrillo, the eminent olive oil producer. I have seen its like made in Sicilian farms, in summer. Crushed tomato pulp is spread outdoors on large boards called *maidde* and allowed to cook down in the sun for three or four days. It is jarred with olive oil and salt, the only other ingredients, besides tomatoes, that are listed on the label. They should also add "sun," because it is what makes Sicilian *strattu* different from other tomato paste. The color is a dark, dark red, the consistency is dense but spoonable, and the taste has a deep tomato aroma, intense and pungent, as of long-cooked sauce.

I don't see why anyone should use tomato paste to fortify a tomato sauce. I make my sauces with genuine San Marzano canned tomatoes, and they need no improvement. In season, I use fresh, ripe Roma tomatoes. I cook them carefully and slowly, and they need no improvement either. Tomato paste is useful to me, if I choose to use it, when I don't have a tomato sauce in the pan, as in a vegetable braise or a stew or a soup. Depending on the flavors of the dish, I'd use either the mild double concentrate from a tube or the Sicilian *strattu*, dissolving it first in a small cup with warm water, broth, or wine, again depending on the flavors of the dish it is going into.

Bottarga

BOTTARGA

Is there anything else taken from the sea that resembles the sweet-salty, musky taste of bottarga, the twin sacs of a gray mullet's eggs, pressed, salted, air-dried, looking like long, large, amber drops? It's a taste of ancient times, the flavor of a technique invented before the Christian era by Phoenician fishermen, or by Arabs. It is from the Arabic that the Italian (and also English) word *bottarga* is derived.

The finest and most expensive bottarga is made in western Sardinia, utilizing gray mullets caught in a brackish lake near Oristano. The two lobes of the mullet's ovaries are gently removed, their natural casing handled carefully to keep the eggs in it intact. The air within the lobes is gently squeezed out, and the flattened lobes are lightly salted and dried in air. When dry, they were once encased and preserved in paraffin or beeswax. Today, they are shipped sealed in the vacuum of plastic packets.

You use bottarga either grated or, like truffles, shaved into thin slices. I make a pasta dish in which it is both grated and sliced. I use the grated for a sauce with garlic, parsley, and olive oil, which I later loosen with a spoonful of hot pasta water. I toss the cooked, drained pasta with the sauce, and I toss it again with bottarga sliced very, very thin and chopped parsley. Either spaghettini—thin spaghetti—or fettuccine work well. Thin shavings of bottarga and spaghetti with clams are a heavenly combination.

In Sardinia, bottarga, in addition to its use over pasta, is either grated or shaved thin, and combined with artichokes— raw, thoroughly trimmed artichoke hearts if served as an antipasto, or sautéed and slivered to make a sauce served over grilled fish.

The most irresistible use of bottarga known to me requires another Sardinian product, *pane carasau*, the round, paper- thin cracker bread also known as sheet music bread. Lightly toast two or more rounds of the bread. It is very brittle; handle it gently as you break it into more or less equal pairs of sandwich-size pieces. Butter each piece on one side with very soft butter. Cover the buttered side with bottarga shav- ings and close the sandwich with its approximately match- ing buttered piece. It could be the most successful appetizer you'll ever serve, but it's painful to have to share it.

Mullet bottarga is also made in Greece, Turkey, and North Africa. It is very inexpensive in Istanbul's bazaars, but nowhere is it as good as Sardinia's. It is now made in Flor- ida's west coast, on the next island to mine. Our waters are rich in gray mullet, which here is also sold smoked. Florida bottarga is excellent, just a little softer and blander than the Sardinian. Many American restaurants are using it.

There is a second type of bottarga made from the roe of another fish that used to be plentiful in the Mediterranean, tuna. It is much larger than mullet bottarga, and after cur- ing, it is cut into small brick-shaped pieces. It is very salty.

When served in thin slices as an appetizer, it is customary to sprinkle lemon juice and olive oil on it. Tuna bottarga is also available grated to use over pasta.

I have been hearing of experiments in the bottarga style using roe from other fish, such as mahimahi, red snapper, and shad. The one I'd be curious to try would be the shad bottarga.

PINE NUTS

I Pinoli

It's not even a nut—it's a little seed—but its place in cooking, in at least one instance, is critical. If you are making pesto, the classic version from Genoa with basil, garlic, olive oil, and cheese, you cannot omit pine nuts. Theirs is the body of the sauce, the resinous fragrance that plays counterpoint to basil's minty scent.

There are many other uses for pine nuts, some of them having infiltrated Italian cooking from the Middle East. I love them with eggplant. I roast the eggplant whole in its skin. When the flesh becomes very soft, the skin collapses, and I pull it away. I toast the pine nuts in butter in a little skillet over medium heat. I must keep turning them, because pine nuts have quite a bit of oil themselves, and if the pan gets too hot they will be scorched. I like them a dark brown, however. I mix them into the soft eggplant flesh together with salt and a few drops of lemon juice and olive oil.

Pine nuts and raisins are a natural match; they are delicious in preparing fresh sardines or small soles in the *saor* style, in which fried fish is covered with a warm marinade of sautéed onions, vinegar, raisins, and pine nuts, then put aside overnight to macerate. Toasted pine nuts add agreeable crunch and nutty flavor to a pasta sauce of sautéed rapini and mashed anchovies. They harmonize with all the green vegetables of southern Italian cooking, with them alone, sautéed with garlic and olive oil and raisins, or all together in a hearty, garlicky sauce for pasta.

Pine nut cookies are a classic with an afternoon cup of espresso. No, not cappuccino, if it's afternoon. My husband's favorite dessert, next to a dark chocolate mousse, is *torta di mandorle con pinoli*, almond cake with pine nuts.

The only unpleasant thing one must say about pinoli is that the top quality—the wonderful, elongated, ivory, intensely fragrant Tuscan pine nuts—are very expensive. So are the Spanish pine nuts, and they are not even as good. Lesser pine nuts, both in price and in tasting quality, are those from America's southwest and from China. They cost about one-fourth of the Italian and Spanish pine nuts.

Refrigerate pine nuts in a tightly covered jar for up to eight months. If you keep them much longer, they will lose fragrance and their oils will begin to turn rancid.

THE SWEET TOOTH

Il Gusto Dolce

In human mouths, there has always been a sweet tooth. Even in the mouths of toothless babes. From our evolutionary beginnings, sweetness is the taste to which we instinctively respond. Cooks have forever sought sources of sweetness. Before sugar became commonly available in Europe, about five hundred years ago, the most important sweeteners were honey and concentrated grape must.

In the kitchen and at table, we have never ceased to make offerings to our sweet tooth. Everyday examples are ketchup, barbecue sauce, Hellmann's mayonnaise, mint jelly with lamb, and uncounted others. There is sugar in our pickled vegetables and fruits and in *agrodolce*, a common sweet-and-sour sauce that Italian cooks make at home. We also continue to turn to such sweet condiments from early times as *saba*, mustard fruits, and balsamic vinegar, all of which are now commercially produced and broadly available.

TRADITIONAL BALSAMIC VINEGAR

Start off with the must—the juice—of freshly crushed Trebbiano white grapes grown in the farmlands of Modena or Reggio Emilia, in northern Italy. Boil it down to a sugary syrup and pour it into the first of what eventually will become a line of five or more barrels, made of different woods in successively decreasing size. In a few years, evaporation will have reduced the contents of the first barrel, which you then transfer to the next smaller barrel in the line. Repeat the procedure until, after a minimum of twelve years, or possibly several decades, you have filled the last and smallest of the barrels. What you will draw from the last barrel, in your time or that of your descendants, is a lustrous nectar of a brown so dark it is nearly indistinguishable from black. It is divinely sweet, but not cloying. It is traditional balsamic vinegar. Depending on its age, a flacon containing approximately three and a half ounces of vinegar may cost up to, or even more than, two hundred dollars.

Traditional balsamic vinegar performs miracles on simple ingredients. Get yourself an eyedropper and use it to dose traditional balsamic on food that is neither strongly spiced nor too creatively encumbered by complicated flavors. A single, fat drop on a sliver of Parmigiano-Reggiano or on a young pecorino such as a marzolino, or on creamy goat cheese. Several drops on strawberries that are already marinated with sugar. Two or three drops on boiled, very fine,

Balsamic vinegars

very fresh green beans that have been tossed with sea salt and extra virgin olive oil. The same on boiled, sliced potatoes. On boiled or baked sliced beets. Some drops on pasta that you are about to toss with a tomato sauce. Two drops on a richly marbled rib eye as it comes off the grill. On liver and bacon. Use traditional balsamic vinegar raw, because cooking silences its more complex and expressive aromas. Sip it out of a small tulip-shaped glass.

Condimento

Condimento balsamico is relatively inexpensive, versatile, and, when bottled by a good producer, a respectable alternative to traditional balsamic. In its finer versions it is composed of young, or even a small quantity of aged, balsamic vinegar made in the traditional manner, blended with unaged, boiled must. The quality of *condimento* can be extremely variable. Look for examples bottled by those who also produce traditional balsamic and who have a reputation to defend. San Giacomo's *condimento* is excellent.

You can use *condimento* more uninhibitedly than you would use a two hundred-dollar bottle of the traditional. In moderate doses, it goes into a marinade for lamb or hoofed game, in sauces and reductions, in a salad, on a risotto with mushrooms. I would counsel restraint, however. Its sweetness can lead to monotony.

Balsamic Vinegar of Modena

There are bottles labeled "balsamic vinegar of Modena," costing twenty-five dollars or more, that deliver a product seeking to evoke something of the taste of traditional balsamic vinegar. They can be useful, but they are exceptions. Most of the vinegar thus labeled is a cheap filler for supermarket shelves, trading on the prestige of traditional balsamic that can cost almost ten times the price. Supermarket balsamic, even if manufactured in Modena, probably contains caramel and sweet thickeners to imitate the natural color, flavor, and consistency of the precious original for which it hopes to be mistaken.

Saba

Saba is a survivor from the epochs when sugar was rare and extremely expensive, and people had to satisfy the craving for sweetness with honey, dates, and syrupy, boiled grape must. It has remained a favorite of country cooks in northern Italy's Emilia-Romagna. *Saba* is usually made from Lambrusco red grapes that are freshly crushed and cooked down to one-third their original volume. It is not aged.

Saba is used to fill a *ciambella* or other homey pastries. It can go sparingly over polenta, and it is most appealing on dry, aged cheeses, as well as on panna cotta or on vanilla gelato—custard cream gelato would be even better.

Saba is available online or in specialty stores, often bottled by a producer of traditional balsamic vinegar.

MOSTARDA DI FRUTTA

Mustard fruit, a product that first became popular in northern Italy in the sixteenth century, consists of fresh, seasonal, and slightly under ripe fruit that is preserved with mustard and sugar. It accompanies either meats or cheese. Some of the meats alongside which you may find a small bowl of mustard fruits are prosciutto cotto, Parma's exquisite cooked ham; cotechino and zampone—creamy, large, steamed pork sausages; cold, sliced rare roast beef; *wurstel,* which is what we call frankfurters in Italy, and smoked pork chops; the magnificent assortment of meats in a *bollito misto,* the mixed boiled meats that in classic northern restaurants are served from the steam compartments of a specially configured trolley and carved tableside.

For nearly every cheese—gorgonzola, both fresh and aged pecorino, robiola, Parmigiano-Reggiano, sheep's milk ricotta, crescenza—you will discover a mustard fruit that fits it. I have a passion for mascarpone with the Veneto's quince mustard.

Nearly every town of the vast northern plain through which the Po River proceeds in its journey eastward to the sea has its own mustard fruit tradition. Quince stars in many of them, and so does pear. Pear mustard is perfect over any firm to hard cheese. The quince mustard from Mantua is an essential component of *tortelli di zucca*, squash-filled pasta dumplings. There is Piedmont's own *mostarda* that contains red grape must, quince, pears, and toasted hazelnuts. The most widely distributed *mostarda* is the one from Cremona, the town more famous abroad for its antique string instruments. Cremona's *mostarda* is characterized by a spicier taste than most of the others and by the use of many different fruits preserved either whole or in large sections.

SALUMI

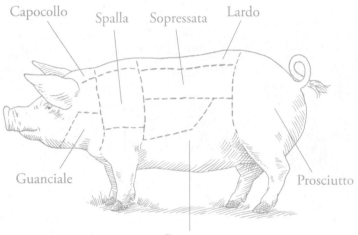

Capocollo   Spalla   Sopressata   Lardo

Guanciale

Prosciutto

Pancetta

PROSCIUTTO CRUDO

Cured Ham

Prosciutto, a product of Nature and craft, is the world's most perfectly created food. Nature furnishes the pig, an animal that surpasses all others in the copious variety of its delectable parts. Artisans take the most precious of those parts, the hind leg, and under the benevolent influence of Nature's other gift, climate, exercise the ancient skill of curing meat with salt and air and time.

You can cook with prosciutto, but it grants its greatest pleasures when you eat it out of hand, sliced fresh from the cured leg, and laid on a single side of buttered, lightly toasted, good plain bread. Also, yes, it is delicious with cantaloupe melon, and heavenly with ripe, ripe figs. My first recollection of a taste I enjoyed goes back to when I was a little girl. It has been almost eighty years, a long reach for taste memory, but I can lucidly remember a slice of Parma ham that the *salumaio* who was serving my mother kindly handed me. Its bright pink color ringed by a glossy white ribbon of sweet fat, the wonder of its luscious, fleshy scent, of the tender, silken meat—if I think of it, I am instantly hungry.

The role of salt in the curing process is to draw away moisture and keep the meat from spoiling while it is curing. *Prosciutto*, the word, comes from the Italian verb *prosciugare*, which means to dry out. Good prosciutto never tastes either salty or dry because of the moist, sweet fat that surrounds it. To strip away that narrow rim of fat is a misguided practice that upends the subtle balance of flavors the curer achieved and prevents prosciutto from delivering the pure pleasure that, after its long, carefully monitored cure, resides within it.

If you have the opportunity, ask the fellow who slices prosciutto if he has the *gambetto*—the end piece toward the shank—available. It is the sweetest and most savory part of the leg. When I can't get to someone who can slice prosciutto fresh for me, I buy one or more of the vacuum-sealed packs of imported Parma ham from the supermarket. The contents are visible, so I go through all the hams in the deli meats counter to pick out the ones that show the most fat.

When you are intending to drape a slice of prosciutto over melon or to wrap it around a honey-oozing fig, it is helpful to have it sliced thin, as long as it's not so thin as to be impalpable. If you are eating it with buttered bread or unsalted crackers, it should be sliced thicker, ideally by hand, to provide more chewy pleasure.

You may want to add the deep flavors of prosciutto to the filling of tortellini or to line a *pasta rotolo*. Prosciutto cut into slivers or sliced thick and diced is the main component of a classic sauce for tagliatelle that the cooks of my hometown make. It is sautéed in unsalted butter at steady, but moderate heat. It mustn't cook long or hard, or it will be too salty. The same caution applies to the Tuscan peas and prosciutto dish. Another prosciutto classic is saltimbocca, in which the sliced ham is pinned with a toothpick to a veal cutlet. In Bologna, prosciutto is wrapped around a small bundle of asparagus, crisscrossed with slices of fontina cheese, and baked.

When prosciutto is cooked, heat dries it out and it becomes saltier, prompting us to reduce or eliminate salt on the other ingredients. On occasion, as I have suggested in some of my recipes, you might consider cooking with prosciutto cotto or plain baked ham instead of cured prosciutto.

PARMA HAM

Wherever someone raises pigs in Italy, someone cures prosciutto. In most instances, the enthusiasm they arouse is not likely to travel far from the production zone, but there are a few whose quality has been widely recognized for centuries. Each prize example of the ham-curing craft can trace some of its distinctive character to the air wherein it spent part of its time. The best known of these is the prosciutto of my childhood memory, the celebrated, salmon-colored Prosciutto di Parma, which for ages has been synonymous with prosciutto itself. The dry, briny air that accompanies the aging of Parma ham is lofted from the Riviera and travels over the hills south and west of Parma, where towns such as Langhirano, at eight hundred feet above sea level, hang their hams during the final months of their cure. Altogether it takes twelve months to cure a Parma ham weighing about twenty-two pounds. An occasional larger ham may cure for up to fourteen months. There are producers who look for legs of special merit in size and quality, which they will age as long as twice the standard time of twelve months. I haven't seen Parma ham aged twenty-four months in any shop here, but if you should find it, that is the one to get. It would be for eating by the slice, not for cooking.

SAN DANIELE

San Daniele's prosciutto is produced in the Friuli-Venezia Giulia region, in the mountainous northeastern edge of Italy. It's a heavier leg than the one used for Parma ham, and it is aged a month or two longer. The trotter is left on, except if shipped to America, when it must be cut off by FDA request. San Daniele is cured high above sea level, where it benefits from an intersection of pine-scented, Alpine airs and the Adriatic's marine breezes. With its sweet flavor, delicately persistent aroma, and all-encompassing Venetian finesse, San Daniele stands apart from other cured hams. You don't want it sliced paper-thin on a machine, but hand-cut and palpable. It needs to be served on a large plate with unsalted butter and grilled bread. Nothing else you would do could increase your enjoyment of it.

CARPEGNA

Another eminent example, Prosciutto di Carpegna, ages for more than a year in the dry, clean air of a small hill town 2,500 feet above sea level. Carpegna, abutted by evergreens and oak trees, the kind of vegetation that flourishes in a dry, cool, mild climate, looks down on the Adriatic from its high perch in the Marche region, close to the Republic of San Marino. In size, color, and flavor, Carpegna's prosciutto resembles Parma's ham more closely than San Daniele's. It is fragrant, sweet, and deep.

CINTA SENESE

Cinta Senese is an odd-looking breed of hog from Tuscany's south. It is black or darkest gray, with a broad white band hugging its shoulders. *Cinta*, the Italian word for "belt," alludes to that white band. In their fourth month, the pigs are let out to roam freely in the woods, where they feed on acorns. When Cinta Senese's dark red flesh, thickly padded with glossy, ivory-white fat, becomes prosciutto, the flavor is extraordinary, intense, sensually stirring, yet fine and fragrantly nutty.

The leg is cured with the trotter on, like San Daniele prosciutto, and aged up to a year and a half. It makes an expensive slice of ham, which travelers to Tuscany can enjoy while the FDA ponders whether it will approve its export to the States.

SAURIS

Smoked ham is a rarity in Italy, a taste associated with Teutonic rather than Latin gastronomy. In the far north of Italy's Friuli-Venezia Giulia region, the remote Sauris valley, which is the source of the country's finest smoked prosciutto, is in fact a German-speaking enclave inside the Italian border. The Sauris production method is drawn both from the Teutonic tradition of spicing and smoking and from the Italian practice of air-drying. The legs to be air-cured are first massaged with a seasoning blend of sea salt, black pepper, and garlic. Using beechwood, they are smoked for no longer than three days, and after a resting period, they are hung to air-dry for at least ten months. The taste of Prosciutto di Sauris, which awaits an export permit, is exquisitely sweet, with smoke just a delicate accent.

SPECK

Speck is produced in Alto Adige/South Tyrol, a formerly Austrian region that became Italian after World War I. Even more than the smoked prosciutto from Sauris, it leans heavily on Teutonic curing tradition, using more spice and more smoke before completing the cure by the Italian air-drying method. The leg that will be made into speck must first be boned and tied, and commercial producers trim away some of the fat. The cured meat is a dark, vivid red against a bright white rim of fat. It is firmer, drier, and more pungently aromatic than Italian-style prosciutto.

PROSCIUTTO COTTO

Cooked Ham

After becoming masters of dry-cured ham, Italians waited several centuries before trying their hand at making cooked ham. It was worth the wait. Prosciutto cotto sets the standard of quality that any ham that is either steamed or boiled would hope to reach. The legs used to make prosciutto cotto come from a hog's hindquarter, like the ones used for curing Parma ham, but they are boned and partially skinned. A proprietary blend of salt and aromatic substances, which varies depending on the producer, is injected into the leg's muscles, then the leg is trimmed to fit a mold wherein it is steamed at moderate temperatures.

A high-quality prosciutto cotto is juicy, tender, fragrant, and appetizingly pink. It gives me as fine a pleasure as the best cured prosciutto. I enjoy mine most when sliced not too thin, with none of its sweet fat removed, and laid on buttered bread.

Prosciutto cotto is invaluable to the cook as a milder alternative to cured prosciutto, which can become quite salty through cooking. I would use it in any sauce that calls for prosciutto, such as the one with prosciutto and asparagus, or in a saltimbocca, or in a baked vegetable dish, or in a frittata.

The best of many producers are Rovagnati Gran Biscotto, Ferrarini, and Parmacotto. Parmacotto has its own New York shop and restaurant, Salumeria Rosi, from which you can order Italian prosciutto cotto online. Rovagnati's Gran Biscotto is also available online, as well as sliced to order at many stores that specialize in Italian products. You may also look online for Ferrarini, which is very highly regarded in Italy both by professionals and consumers.

Guanciale

GUANCIALE

I wasn't raised to cook with guanciale. I didn't even know it existed. When I was young, I assumed, like other Italians, that there wasn't anything worth knowing about food beyond the dishes that Mother brought to the table. Everything I have learned since, aside from my family's cooking, I have learned by living in many different places. In Italy, a different place is different in everything: in its appearance, in its dialect, in the history of its people, and strikingly, in its cooking. When, in the 1960s, my husband and I moved to Rome, I made guanciale's acquaintance, and along with it came the experience of a bold cuisine with rich, palate-stunning flavor.

Guanciale is the jowl of a nine-month-old pig, rubbed with salt, black pepper, and other spices, and air-dried for three months. It is often compared to pancetta, which undergoes a comparable cure, but it is firmer and more richly endowed with tasty fat, and the flavor it contributes to the dishes where it is present is more intense than pancetta.

Guanciale is an indivisible part of such iconic Roman pastas as carbonara, amatriciana, and *gricia*. It is also essential to vegetables such as fava beans braised in the Roman manner with olive oil. If you are among those who appreciate the luscious texture and flavor of tripe, *trippa alla romana* with mint and guanciale will make you happy. If you are making a *battuto* mincing celery, onion, carrot, and parsley and you want to add intensity to it, you could use guanciale. Wrap very thin slices of guanciale around peeled, marinated shrimp and grill over a moderate fire. Delicious. When making a sauce with prosciutto dice, you may sometimes replace the prosciutto with similarly diced guanciale. Guanciale sliced thin can be crisped as you would bacon. My husband nibbles it as he slices it. If it has been fully cured, it is safe to eat uncooked, like prosciutto.

Guanciale in America is necessarily different from guanciale in Italy. Italian butchers use hogs that are at least nine months old and weigh more than 350 pounds. The hogs butchered in the States are no older than six months, and when slaughtered, weigh about 270 pounds. The quality of the meat in the much smaller American guanciale, the balance between well-developed fat and muscle heft, falls short of the Roman original.

The flavor of American guanciale may not quite equal the Italian model, but even at the commercial level there is acceptable guanciale available in this country, both online and from food stores that specialize in Italian products. If you have access to a good, and possibly older and heavier hog, you may even decide to make it yourself, following the recipes posted on the Internet. It shouldn't be too difficult.

PANCETTA

Pancetta translates as "little belly." It is made, indeed, from the half fat and half lean meat of a pig's belly. Pancetta is salted, spiced, and air-cured for three weeks to three months, depending on the cure and the curer. It enjoys a broader welcome in American kitchens than any other Italian pork product, and well-deserved it is. Sliced or diced or chopped fine, depending on the recipe, its balanced flavor enriches dishes beyond counting in cuisines both in and out of Italian tradition.

Nothing like a thin slice of pancetta works so well in making rollups, best with veal, but delicious with any meat scaloppini. When skewering delicate seafood such as scallops or shrimp for the grill, a strip of pancetta pinned to each piece with a toothpick will enhance it with moisture and flavor. Diced pancetta is divine intervention in the cooking of vegetables, and heaven-sent in pasta sauces. If you can't get your hands on guanciale, pancetta is an irreproachable substitute in a carbonara or an amatriciana. Add a grating of Parmigiano and black pepper to eggs and pancetta to make a frittata that achieves absolute goodness.

Pancetta comes either flat—*stesa*—or rolled up—*arrotolata.* I prefer the rolled-up version, the more popular one in northern Italy, because I find it moister and sweeter. It doesn't take me long to go through a whole pancetta, particularly if I find the delicious one that Paul Bertolli makes at Fra' Mani in Berkeley. I keep it refrigerated, tightly wrapped in aluminum foil. When I am out of his and need pancetta, I get it from the supermarket, sliced thick or thin as I may require. If you don't use all your sliced pancetta right away, lay the slices flat on a sheet of aluminum foil, arranging them side by side with minimal overlapping. Place another sheet of foil on top and flatten it with a rolling pin or a bottle to force out all the air you can. Fold over the edges of the foil. You should be able to see the profile of each slice bulging against the foil. This is a neat way to keep leftover slices of prosciutto or mortadella or other sliced meats.

Pancetta Affumicata

In Venice, where I once lived, and elsewhere in the Veneto region and in the other regions of northeastern Italy, smoked pancetta is as common as the more Italian salt-cured version. It is a gastronomic souvenir of the nineteenth-century Austrian occupation.

Carnesecca

If you travel to Tuscany, *carnesecca* is what native Tuscans call pancetta. A Tuscan product called *rigatino* is similar to pancetta. It is made from the flank of the pig, salted and rubbed with pepper, garlic, rosemary, and ground lemon and orange rind. It is rolled up like pancetta and aged for about a month and a half.

Caul fat

CAUL FAT

La Rete di Maiale

Anyone who has overcooked a fish fillet, or has been faced with a discouragingly lean piece of pork loin or venison, or has had game birds to roast, or is weary of the dryness of chicken breasts, or would like her hamburger to have a more luxurious feel, any cook at all needs caul fat in her kitchen.

Caul is a lacy membrane of pure fat that shelters the organs of a pig's abdominal cavity. It is as pretty as a doily and does wonders wrapped around a piece of meat. While the meat cooks, the caul around it melts and vanishes, leaving behind it moistness and good flavor.

In Italian cooking, the most celebrated use of caul fat is with *fegatelli* (pork liver). Cut fresh pork liver into stubby, sausage-like chunks, sprinkle with salt, lay a bay leaf on each chunk, and wrap it a couple of times with a piece of caul. Grill over charcoal, just long enough for the caul to melt, which it does quickly. I adore liver, and of the many things I can do with it, *fegatelli* with caul fat is the one I love best.

Caul fat is soft and flexible. Cut it to fit and wrap it around anything you want to bake, roast, or fry. Drape it on the breast of a chicken you are roasting, wrap a whole quail with it, line a gratin pan in which you will bake vegetables or wrap it around the vegetables themselves, use it as a more practical and edible sausage casing, enclose mashed potatoes in a square of caul to make fritters, bandage a leg of lamb with caul, or enclose a whole meat loaf.

Before you use it, soften caul fat for about ten minutes in lukewarm water and rinse it with vinegar to chase away any funkiness. Soak it briefly in water again afterward.

You are likely to be buying caul fat frozen. It stays in excellent condition in the freezer for several weeks. If possible, thaw only what you are going to use. If you must thaw it all, spread the caul flat and roll it up lined with plastic wrap for storage in the refrigerator. If you have a butcher that can provide you with fresh caul fat, line it with plastic wrap and store it until you need it. It should keep well in the refrigerator for two to three weeks.

COTECHINO AND ZAMPONE

Cotechino and its twin, zampone, are large pork sausages whose delectable creamy consistency, when they have been cooked, comes from the large percentage of ground pork rind in the composition of their stuffing. *Cotica* is the Italian word for pork rind or skin, hence the name of the sausage, *cotechino.* Zampone is the pig's trotter, scooped hollow and filled like cotechino with a ground-up mixture of pork shoulder, neck, and other lean cuts, fatback, and pork rind. They were created in Modena province at the time of the Renaissance and have remained among the most delicious of northern Italian pork products for five hundred years. Cotechino came first, soon followed by zampone.

When fully cooked, pork rind becomes gelatinous. It is said that one can tell if a cotechino contains the necessary amount of gelatin when your fingers become sticky touching a cooked slice of it. Cooks in Italy capitalize on the succulent, buttery character of pork rind by using it in stews, soups, and a casserole of cannellini or cranberry beans; cutting into a fine dice and adding it to the filling of stuffed vegetables; or even by cooking the rind to soften it and making stuffed meat rollups with broad strips of it.

In northern Italy one celebrates New Year's Day at

home with reddish pink slices of a boiled cotechino—or zampone—spread on a platter alongside a mound of lentils that are a metaphor for coins, hence prosperity. A sliced cotechino or two is the starring event of a Sunday with the family in winter, served with mashed potatoes, or polenta, or sautéed Savoy cabbage, or alone with mustard fruits. In Venice, where it is called *musetto*, the creamiest of all cotechinos, one of our favorite winter *cicchetti*—Venetian tapas served at wine bars—was a steaming slice of cotechino served over a round of bread or a square of grilled polenta and topped with mustard.

There are varying approaches to cooking a whole cotechino, but all agree that it has to start in cold water and it must boil at a simmer for about two hours. I like to let it soak in cold water first for at least a few hours, or even overnight. Some puncture the casing first with toothpicks and cook it wrapped in muslin. I do not.

It may not be easy to find butchers that make fresh cotechino, and when they do, they rarely endow it with its traditional full complement of ground pork rind so that, once cooked, it ends up with the consistency of boiled salami. What you can find easily at online sources is fully cooked, creamy cotechino imported from Italy and packed in a sealed foil bag. Boil the cotechino in that bag for about thirty minutes, checking the package instructions. Once done, retrieve the bag using tongs, place it in a deep dish, and snip open one end, emptying out the hot fluids it contains. Slide the cotechino out of its foil bag and onto a serving platter, where you can slice it. Handle it carefully; the hot, moist sausage is very slippery, and it could slide right off of the platter and onto the floor, as has once happened to me.

LARDO

Lardo is what you make to capitalize on the sweet taste and luscious texture of the most delectable part of the pig: its fat. Lardo is not the rendered fat used for frying; it is a solid piece of pure, uncooked fat cured with salt, garlic, herbs, and spices for a period that, depending on where it is made and by whom, may last from a few weeks to two years. The fat for lardo, a layer about one and a half inches thick, is taken from the pig's back, preferably from over its hindquarters. It is cured with sea salt, black pepper, rosemary, and chopped garlic and aged in a tightly closed container.

The lardo that you buy in the States is produced here. Many chefs make their own. If you travel to Italy, it would be worth your time to taste lardo in its country of origin, particularly that produced in two small zones whose lardo is extraordinary and inimitable. The more famous of the two is in Colonnata, a mountain town in Tuscany, adjacent to Carrara and its historic quarries of white marble.

Colonnata cures its lardo in small, sarcophagus-like tubs made from locally quarried marble. The internal surfaces of the tub are rubbed with garlic. Slabs of lard are rubbed with salt and tightly packed inside the tub, each slab resting on a mixture of salt, black pepper, rosemary, and garlic, and occasionally, depending on the producer, one or two other less traditional herbs. A solid marble lid is lowered onto the tub, sealing it tightly. Inside, the lardo cures for six months to a year. A two-year curing period is not unknown, but it has become rare. The salt draws out moisture, submerging the lard in a protective brine that keeps it from spoiling. The fine grain of the marble of the curing tubs creates a unique aging environment wherein the scents released by the herbs and spices gently infiltrate the lardo.

The itinerary of your trip to Italy may not include the Valle d'Aosta, an Alpine region on the border with France, but it is worth a detour for its landscape, its dishes, its ethereal wines, and its special lardo, Lardo d'Arnad. The fat comes from the shoulders of pigs that have never eaten grain, but only chestnuts and local greens. The curing brine with which the slabs of lard are covered is seasoned with sea salt, rosemary, bay leaves, sage, nutmeg, juniper berries, cloves, and garlic. The traditional curing container, called a *doil*, was, until recently, handmade of chestnut wood. It is being replaced by glass boxes in which Lardo d'Arnad ages for twelve months to two years. If the producer chooses to age it two years, he will make the brine with white wine. The finely aromatic flavor of Lardo d'Arnad is more intense than Lardo di Colonnata, yet delicate withal.

The universal way of enjoying lardo is to slice it very thin—the effortless passage of a sharp blade going through lardo is itself a tactile pleasure—and then lay it, with a light grinding of black pepper, on still-hot grilled bread. When it meets the heat of the bread, the lardo immediately begins to dissolve.

Other delicious uses abound for lardo: draped over a lamb chop as you turn it over on a grill; accompanying warm butter beans; as a wrap when grilling shelled lobster tails or large shrimp that you have previously marinated with salt, lemon juice, bread crumbs, and olive oil; with a ripe pear; over roasting potatoes. Sliced or thickly diced, you can command the soft touch and lightly spiced scent of lardo to delight you in infinite combinations with meat, seafood, crusty breads, pizza, *pasta e fagioli*, fresh cheeses, and fried eggs.

Cunza, Crema di Lardo

In the countryside kitchens of Emilia-Romagna, women make a scone-like salty biscuit called *tigella*, which they slice open and stuff with a cream of whipped lardo known as *cunza*. The other components, beside lardo (some cooks use pancetta instead of lardo), are salt, pepper, rosemary, and garlic. Very little garlic. The narrowest hole of a meat grinder is the best tool through which to grind all the ingredients, but if you don't have a meat grinder, patiently mince the rosemary leaves and garlic very, very fine using a sharp chef's knife or a mezzaluna, then whip everything up together with the lardo (or pancetta) in a food processor. Spoon the cream on bruschetta or on meat on the grill or on a roast loin of pork. When stuffing it into *tigelle*, Bolognese cooks add a grating of Parmigiano-Reggiano.

ACKNOWLEDGMENTS

Susan Moldow, president of the Scribner Publishing Group, was in it from the beginning. In fact, she *was* the beginning. It was Susan who said to Marcella at dinner, here you are, always talking about ingredients, why don't you write a guide to them for people to use? Marcella did and it was the final satisfying project of her teaching career. Thank you, Susan.

That Kara Watson became the last of the many editors who have been associated with Marcella's writings is an event both providential and ironic. Ironic that it came only at the end of a long career, providential that this valedictory work was shepherded by a woman so warmly endowed with editorial virtues, steadfastly supportive and protective of our aims, patiently yet keenly watchful over our path, clearing it of obstructions, blocking digressions, tightening our focus when it began to waver. Thank you, Kara.

Karin Lubart illustrated Marcella's magnum opus, *Essentials of Classic Italian Cooking*, when it was published in 1992. Twenty-three years later, Kara Watson tracked her down in Tennessee and persuaded her to illustrate *Ingredienti*. We are so glad she did, bringing to her subjects the affection that Marcella herself felt for her ingredients. Thank you, Karin.

ONLINE SOURCES

GUSTIAMO.COM

My basic resource for high-quality imported Italian pantry components. There I get genuine San Marzano tomatoes, Martelli pasta, some olive oils, bottarga, anchovy colatura, and *u stratto*, Sicilian tomato concentrate, among other specialties. Just before Thanksgiving, they bring in a panettone that is as moist and light as the one we used to buy from an artisan baker in Milan every Christmas.

CHEFSHOP.COM

I have shopped this Seattle grocer longer than I have used any other online source. They have excellent Italian oils, pasta, and mountain-grown Parmigiano-Reggiano and a large variety of both local and global foods. I keep a supply of their June Taylor jams, and what I am particularly grateful for is their fresh wild salmon and their Washington State cherries and hardneck garlic.

ALMAGOURMET.COM

Dried Sicilian herbs on their branches, Calabrian chili pepper, Gragnano pasta, fresh or frozen whole porcini mushrooms, and precooked cotechino sausage are among their vast selection of Italian specialties. What I find most alluring are the fresh Italian vegetables that Alma offers in season, such as late-harvest radicchio and puntarelle.

GOURMET-DELIGHTS.COM

Jeff Pfohl's site is crammed with intriguing items from Italy and other Mediterranean regions. I go there for seven-year-old Acquerello Carnaroli, a rice that, when it comes to making risotto, has no equal.

FORMAGGIOKITCHEN.COM, MURRAYSCHEESE.COM, IDEALCHEESE.COM, IGOURMET.COM, OLIOANDOLIVE.COM, BUONITALIA.COM, ZINGERMANS.COM, THEROGERSCOLLECTION.COM

Purveyors of artisanal foods and most valuable as sources of mountain-grown, superior-quality, long-aged Parmigiano-Reggiano.

FRAMANI.COM AND SALUMERIABIELLESE.COM

In my experience, the two American producers of cured pork specialties that most closely approach the flavor of the Italian originals on which they are modeled. The Salumeria Biellese's Felino-style salami and its guanciale are among the most admirable of its many other cured meats. At Fra' Mani, Paolo Bertolli's pancetta, his salame gentile and salame nostrano do not fear comparison with Italy's best. Neither producer fulfills retail orders from its website, but they will tell you which local or online purveyor carries their products. Salumeria Biellese's specialties are also available in its New York shop, at 378 Eighth Avenue. There are, moreover, Italian salumi makers who have brought their skills and traditional recipes to this country, where they are creating cured pork products with genuine Italian flavor.

FILIPPO GAMBASSI AND CESARE CASELLA

While waiting for their websites to go up, these two young Tuscan producers on the scene will fill orders sent to their email addresses: INFO@TERRADISIENAUSA.COM for Filippo Gambassi and INFO.GIORGIOSALAMI@GMAIL.COM for Cesare Casella. To your list of online salumi, you might add OLIOANDOLIVE.COM, a general site mentioned above. They carry an excellent American-made Felino salame.

URBANI.COM AND REGALISFOODS.COM

The most reliable I have used for white and black truffles. Regalis is also a source of choice fresh wild mushrooms. I have found that in ordering truffles, it is helpful to speak to a manager of the site. At Urbani, I write or talk to Nazzareno Miele. There can be huge variables in quality that depend on personal attention to the order, or lack of it.

ANNAMARIAFISHCOMPANY.COM

Mullet bottarga imported from Sardinia (Gustiamo is a reliable purveyor) is the standard for this delicacy made of pressed and dried gray mullet roe, but gray mullet is also abundant in the waters of the Gulf of Mexico, in Southwest Florida. The Anna Maria Fish Company produces bottarga from their roe that compares creditably with the original Sardinian specialty.

KINGARTHURFLOUR.COM

Italian-style 00 flour for homemade egg tagliatelle and other cuts that have the lightness, buoyancy, and flavor of pasta in Bologna. This is also my source for the unbleached cotton cheesecloth with which I wrap and store hunks of Parmigiano-Reggiano, so much better than the loose, raggedy cheesecloth from the supermarket.

FORMATICUM.COM

Use their cheese paper and bags to protect the flavor and extend the life of cheeses other than Parmigiano-Reggiano that you store in the refrigerator.

DAPHNISANDCHLOE.COM

Marvelous herbs from ancient Greek sites, smartly packed and mailed directly from Greece.